Adaptable Project Management

A combination of Agile and Project Management for All (PM4A)

Adaptable Project Management

A combination of Agile and Project Management for All (PM4A)

COLIN BENTLEY

it gp™

IT Governance Publishing

IT Governance Publishing Ltd
Unit 3, Clive Court
Bartholomew's Walk
Cambridgeshire Business Park
Ely, Cambridgeshire
CB7 4EA
United Kingdom
www.itgovernancepublishing.co.uk

First published in the United Kingdom in 2020 by IT Governance Publishing.

ISBN 978-1-78778-231-0

ABOUT THE AUTHOR

Colin Bentley is the author of the original PRINCE2® manual for the Central Computer and Telecommunications Agency (CCTA). He was the Chief Examiner for the Association for Project Management Group and the CCTA until his retirement.

Colin has had more than 20 books published, has lectured widely on project management and has acted as project management consultant to such firms as The London Stock Exchange, Microsoft® Europe, Tesco Stores, Commercial Union and the BBC.

Colin has been working with PRINCE2®, PRINCE® and its predecessor, PROMPT II, since 1975 and was part of the team that created the original method.

Colin created the PM4A project management method for smaller projects. Feeling that a better method could be found by combining this 'waterfall' method of project management with Agile principles, he has now written *Adaptable Project Management*, a comprehensive method for handling any size of project, especially those where the scope and detail cannot be seen at the beginning.

ACKNOWLEDGEMENTS

My thanks to Andy Britton for his faith in me, and to John Fisher for his thoughtful input.

For a long time I have thought about the Parable of the Talents in Matthew 25:14–30, and wondered how I could return to the Lord more talents than I was given. Maybe I'm wrong, but writing seems to me the best talent that I have been given, so I dedicate this book to the Lord in the hope that it will be judged some kind of return on the talents that he has given me.

I would also like to thank Christopher Wright and Prasad Lele, for their helpful comments during the production of this book.

> "I love deadlines. I love the whooshing noise they make as they go by."
>
> **Douglas Adams, *The Salmon of Doubt*, Macmillan, 2002.**

DISCLAIMER

All names and examples quoted in this book are fictitious and have been presented solely for learning, understanding and explaining purposes.

PREFACE

Adaptable Project Management (APM) is my name for the merging of PM4A, a more traditional waterfall project management method, with *some* aspects of Agile that I think work well in combination,, such as evolutionary development, iteration, timeboxing and communication.

Waterfall methods such as PM4A have been around since the 1960s, whereas some of the key aspects of Agile have only been around since the 1990s. There are now several versions of Agile.

If we are to effectively combine the many excellent features of a good waterfall method of project management with the iterative approach of Agile, then 'something has to give'. What you will see in this book is a modification of some aspects of traditional project management in order to take advantage of the many good points available in Agile.

I have taken some decisions as to which parts of the various Agile offerings to include. One that I like a lot is the Dynamic System Development Method (DSDM) Atern version of Agile, and I would like to acknowledge my inclusion of its eight principles and some of its sensible words.

This is not intended to be 'full Agile'. I think Agile has too many technical terms and is still too wedded to software development to be a genuine all-purpose project management method. I have created something new to be what I think a generic project management method should be, so I have deliberately omitted 'Agile' from the book's main title. I include a lot of chapters that I think are good and better than any found elsewhere. The modifications are mine, so don't get overheated if you don't find technical terms like 'Scrum'. Just read it for what it is.

CONTENTS

Chapter 1: Introduction to adaptable project management..1

Chapter 2: Agile terminology 13

Chapter 3: Case study 21

Chapter 4: Principles 25

Chapter 5: Organisation...............................33

Chapter 6: Planning.............................49

Chapter 7: Risk 65

Chapter 8: Change........................79

Chapter 9: Progress 105

Chapter 10: Techniques 115

Chapter 11: Introduction to the processes.............147

Chapter 12: The *Propose* phase 151

Chapter 13: The *Plan* phase............................161

Chapter 14: The *Create* phase............................171

Chapter 15: The *Close* phase 181

Appendix A.1: Action Log............................189

Appendix A.2: Daily log 191

Appendix A.3: Post project review plan 193

Appendix A.4: Problem report 195

Appendix A.5: Product description.........................197

Appendix A.6: Product version control 199

Appendix A.7: Progress report........................201

Appendix A.8: Project closure report 203

Appendix A.9: Project issue 205

Contents

Appendix A.10: Project justification 207

Appendix A.11: Project mandate 211

Appendix A.12: Project proposal 213

Appendix A.13: Risk report 215

Appendix A.14: Work package 217

Further reading 219

CHAPTER 1: INTRODUCTION TO ADAPTABLE PROJECT MANAGEMENT

1.1 Who is this book aimed at?

Project managers and stakeholders trying to develop a project management approach suitable for their organisation. Many staff are expected to take on project manage mentor 'client/product owner' roles without any briefing or other support. This book will help to address this gap. It will also benefit any readers doing a project assurance review for the first time.

1.2 Background

I don't want to confuse readers. I understand that 'Evo – Evolutionary Project Management' is a term used by Tom Gilb and his partners. I was introduced to Tom Gilb's ideas back in the 1960s and greatly admired his thinking, but this is not a book based on his 'Evo'. It is a combination of the old 'waterfall' methods of project management, such as PRINCE2® and PM4A, and the Agile method of software development.

1.3 'Waterfall' project development

'Waterfall' is a name given to 'traditional' projects that follow the format of specify, design, develop, deliver. It is assumed that all the requirements can be defined at the outset and that nothing (or almost nothing) will be delivered to the client until the project finishes.

Project Management for All (PM4A) is a method I created with Andy Britton in the early 2000s. Itis a simple but comprehensive method of project management based on the waterfall method. PM4A is aimed at smaller projects and is very strong in the areas of starting up a project and providing an in-depth view of how to handle quality, risk, version and change control.

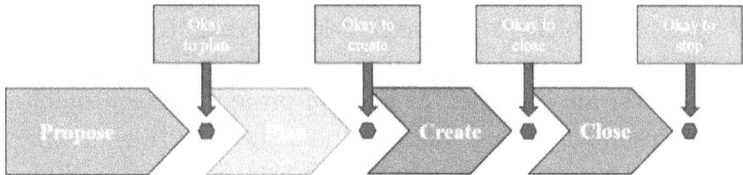

Figure 1.1: PM4A phases

1.4 Agile project management

Agile project management is an iterative approach to delivering useful parts of the product of a project throughout its life cycle.

Iterative or Agile life cycles are composed of several iterations or incremental steps towards the completion of a project. Iterative approaches are frequently used in software development projects to promote early delivery of key components and adaptability. The benefit of iteration is that you can adjust as you go along rather than having to follow a linear path. One of the aims of an Agile or iterative approach is to release benefits throughout the process rather than only at the end. Popular methods for Agile software development include Scrum, Lean, Dynamic System Development Method (DSDM) and Extreme Programming (XP).

Although Agile started out as a method purely for software development, it is now often used for non-software projects.

The 'Agile Manifesto' came out of a meeting of software developers in 2001 in Snowbird, Utah. It was based on work that had been going on since around 1994 around a growing need for a robust approach to software development that could deliver benefits as early as possible. I can remember working with Tom Gilb back in the 1960s when he was already working on 'evolutionary development', very much ahead of his time with this Agile concept.

I believe the first to call themselves 'Agile' were early Toyota teams who added frequent customer feedback to their work.

1.4.1 The Agile Manifesto

As a background to this book, the following is the 2001 Agile Manifesto:

> We are uncovering better ways of developing software by doing it and helping others to do it. Through this work we have come to value:
>
> - **Individuals and interactions** over processes and tools
> - **Working software** over comprehensive documentation
> - **Customer collaboration** over contract negotiation
> - **Responding to change** over following a plan.
>
> That is, while there is value in the items on the right, we value the items on the left more.[1]

---

[1]*https://agilemanifesto.org/*.

1.4.2 Principles behind the Agile Manifesto

Our highest priority is to satisfy the customer through early and continuous delivery of valuable software.

Welcome changing requirements, even late in development. Agile processes harness change for the customer's competitive advantage.

Deliver working software frequently, from a couple of weeks to a couple of months, with a preference to the shorter timescale.

Business people and developers must work together daily throughout the project.

Build projects around motivated individuals. Give them the environment and support they need, and trust them to get the job done.

The most efficient and effective method of conveying information to and within a development team is face-to-face conversation.

Working software is the primary measure of progress.

Agile processes promote sustainable development. The sponsors, developers, and users should be able to maintain a constant pace indefinitely.

Continuous attention to technical excellence and good design enhances agility.

Simplicity--the art of maximizing the amount of work not done--is essential.

The best architectures, requirements, and designs emerge from self-organizing teams.

At regular intervals, the team reflects on how to become more effective, then tunes and adjusts its behavior accordingly.[2]

We can see the background of software development very clearly in these principles. One of the tasks I cover in this book is to turn a method specifically designed for software development into a generic one that can be applied to a variety of industries.

Although this manifesto is enticing for anyone looking to manage the development of a project, Agile has received criticism over the years:

Agile drawbacks

- More suited to continuous development (i.e. there is a never-ending stream of changes, so where does the project stop?).
- Can get out of control (if you break the rules; e.g. Agile allows no time slippage to complete a piece of allocated work. If this rule is broken and work continues beyond its current time limit until the work is finished, the schedule is ruined and other packages that are meant to coincide with it are also affected. Agile is built around stopping work when the time runs out and returning anything unfinished to the work queue to be re-prioritised).
- Can be difficult to give an early idea of total cost (how easy is it to estimate how many changes will be

---

[2] *https://agilemanifesto.org/principles.html*.

requested, compared to senior management wanting a clear idea of project cost at the outset?).

- Work is deferred from an iteration and never gets completed. This can be a common problem for security and control features.
- Requires users to fully engage and be disciplined.
- Requires a 'no blame' culture.

However, for the all the criticism, Agile has some great features which can be adapted to projects in multiple industries:

Agile benefits

- Delivers real business benefits, not unnecessary fluff.
- Deeply involves users in the development process.
- Users feel involved and empowered.
- Gives early visibility of working prototypes.
- Receive early user feedback.
- Reduces testing and defects.
- Reduces unnecessary processes and documentation.
- Lessens management overhead.
- **Delivers on time!**

1.5 The different approaches

Agile basic philosophy is that any project must:

- Be aligned to clearly defined strategic goals; and
- Focus on early delivery of real benefits to the business.

This is best achieved when key stakeholders understand the business objectives, are empowered to an appropriate level and collaborate with solution developers and each other to deliver the right solution in the agreed timescales, according to priorities set by the business.

Agile's roots are in IT development, and much of the documentation around still refers to software development, but supporters of Agile now believe that it can be used for any type of project. This book is based on the belief that it can be universal if supported by **certain PM4A proven ideas.**

Agile is based on iteration and incremental progress, and focuses on adaptability to changing product requirements and enhancing customer satisfaction through rapid delivery of working product features and client participation. This is a major difference to traditional 'waterfall' development, where changes after the initial specification are regarded as a threat because a lot of emphasis is placed on a clearly defined project plan that asks for a budget commitment at the end of initiation, with the expectation that the project should come in close to that figure. Agile's initiation plan will be a far more open-ended figure, with the expectation that more detail and change will appear as the project progresses. The project plan – sometimes known as the delivery plan –and, therefore, the budget for it, gradually evolves as more is known. An Agile initiation plan's focus is more on what is wanted as opposed to how it will be provided.

An Agile life cycle is very different to traditional 'waterfall' development frameworks.

```
┌─────────────────┐
│   Requirements  │
│    gathering    │
└────────┬────────┘
         ▼
┌─────────────────┐
│      Design     │
└────────┬────────┘
         ▼
┌─────────────────┐
│   Development   │
└────────┬────────┘
         ▼
┌─────────────────┐
│  System testing │
└────────┬────────┘
         ▼
┌─────────────────┐
│    Delivery /   │
│   deployment    │
└─────────────────┘
```

Figure 1.2: Waterfall development

Agile expects requirements to evolve and change. Time may be fixed for the life of the project and resources fixed as far as possible. Flexibility comes from the ability to prioritise requirements as they are elicited during the early project stages and as they are refined during the project lifecycle.

To understand the entire Agile cycle in a nutshell, cross-functional teams work simultaneously to develop the products in a series of 'timeboxes'. Each Agile timebox[3] traditionally lasts from one to two months. Current trends indicate that in certain projects they may last from just seven to ten days, but remember that this may apply to software development rather than other types of project.

At the end of each timebox, the development of a working product feature has been iterated until releasable and presented to the product owner for verification purposes. The entire process is repeated through timeboxes until all the product features are developed.

In Agile, more emphasis is given to the sustained and rapid development of product features rather than spending time at the beginning trying to complete the analysis of all the requirements and initial project planning, i.e. deliver something working, sooner rather than later. Besides the actual solution development, other aspects of project work such as product analysis, prototypes, detailed specification and design of product features, developing the functionality and 'testing' the development for errors are also carried out by means of timeboxes as the project progresses.

In most Agile environments people work in teams. Self-organisation and motivation take precedence over delegation of authority and following the 'seniority' hierarchy. Team members are all encouraged to take an active part in the development and planning activities. Agile teams have enough autonomy to own how they do their work. The Agile team must collaborate and share ideas to develop the product.

A representative of the customer (product owner) is part of each development team and approves the product features as they are developed through the timebox cycles. A lot of time

---

[3] See section 2.9 for a definition of 'timebox'.

is saved through this customer collaboration, and as a result, the project proceeds smoothly and more quickly than in environments where the customers are kept at arm's length (I knew a few of these in the old days!).

Agile focuses on incorporating dynamic changes in the product development cycle. Changes in the product features can be easily and effortlessly carried out by developing 'user stories' – product functionality or features as defined in the product Prioritised Requirements List (PRL) or product backlog. Changes can be carried out at any time while the features are being developed – even late in the product development cycle. The danger here, of course, is that a project never finishes, because changes and new requirements continue to stream in.

Agile processes make extensive use of events such as daily team meetings and retrospective meetings to check progress and identify and self-correct the development process carried out by the team. Feedback is solicited frequently from the stakeholders to collaborate and speed up the development process through the sharing of ideas and self-management.

1.6 Complement or clash?

As we have just read, one of the key concepts of Agile is the building of the end product in a series of iterations; build a bit, find out a bit more about what you've done and what is required next, add a bit more and so on round the building loop until the product is finished.

So, do we simply have two widely different approaches to projects? Do we choose one or the other? Or is there a middle road, where we can merge the two to make an even more powerful method of managing projects? I hope that's where this book comes in.

Both see the business need/justification as important, so that's a good start. Also, both have a strong emphasis on quality, though they have different approaches to it. No doubt these can be built into a very strong handle on quality.

There is some common ground between the Agile concept of build incrementally and develop iteratively and the PM4A 'Plans' principle. They address different aspects of planning, but we will see that these can be complementary, not adversarial. The basic approach to planning by focusing on products, rather than activities, supports the quality approach and gives a very solid base to any planning.

The Agile principles of collaboration and continuous communication fit in with traditional progress control, and make it much easier than taking the time to create formal progress reports.

There is also a lot of common ground between Agile's acceptance of change and the 'Change control' principle of PM4A, but we need to be careful here. By continuing to accept changes and new requirements, many Agile projects move without interruption into what traditional project management would call maintenance and enhancement. This works fine where you have, for example, a software system looking after an aspect of hospital work. Work there is never-ending, with new requirements coming along in an endless stream. Where 'waterfall' methods would be looking for a finite end point, Agile copes with an open-ended requirement quite easily. We will be looking for a method that can handle a clear end point yet still provide a means to incorporate changes.

Although project roles are not part of the Agile principles, perhaps they should be, because Agile offers a very comprehensive role structure. Our method must produce an organisational structure from the Agile and the very simple PM4A offerings.

Three things stand out. There is no PM4A equivalent of the Agile 'deliver on time', and this is something that can be brought into a combination of the two methods. In PM4A, the risk subject is more comprehensively dealt with and product-based planning can be very helpful. Both are important and will add greatly to a combination of the two methods. Some Agile offerings touch on the need for version control, but I believe that the procedures for this need to be much more comprehensive. The PM4A approach to change must be more flexible to accommodate Agile principles, but we must recognise that some suggested changes may be so big that senior management need to be involved in any decision making.

In this book, I am going to adapt the PM4A method to create a method of flexible project management. I shall call this powerhouse, 'Adaptable Project Management' (APM).

1.7 The way ahead

Following the next chapter on terminology, the remainder of the book will present a method of project management that I believe incorporates the best of both methods. This is where APM starts.

Throughout this book, I will explain:

1. This is what Agile says.
2. This is what PM4A says.
3. The difference (if there is one) matters because ...
4. Here is what I think (my) APM should do.

CHAPTER 2: AGILE TERMINOLOGY

2.1 Artefacts

In Agile-speak, artefacts are products. Agile talks about six 'common' artefacts. In PM4A terms, these artefacts are project management products.

The six common artefacts are:

Product vision statement

The **vision statement** is a 'what we are trying to achieve' **statement** that the development team, **Scrum** Master and stakeholders refer to throughout the project. Anyone involved with the project, from the development team to the CEO, should be able to understand the **product vision statement**. In PM4A this might be the project mandate.

Product roadmap

A **product roadmap** is a high-level visual summary that maps out the vision and direction of your **product** offering over time. A **product roadmap** communicates the why and what behind what you are building. It is a guiding strategic document as well as a plan for executing the strategy. In PM4A there is the project justification document.

Release plan

Project plan.

Product backlog

A list of all the products needed for the end product.

In PM4A the first of these would be called the project plan and, using product-based planning, the product backlog would be shown in the product breakdown structure.

Sprint backlog

In PM4A the equivalent would be a plan for the *Create* phase.

Increment (timebox)

In PM4A this would be a work package.

2.2 Information radiator

A general term used to describe the use of noticeboards containing information that can be readily accessed by people working on the project. Information radiators should be big, visible, unavoidable and able to convey information at a glance from across the room.

An information radiator can contain any information, and it typically shows such things as work to do (the PRL), work in progress and how work is progressing. If we enlarge this concept to include identified risks and issues, the PM4A action log for these becomes more open. Such boards often include policies for changes of work states. The concept is to have this information available on physical noticeboards for all to see, rather than in electronic form where visibility is less easy to achieve.

2.3 Iterative development

You might think that in general, an iteration is the act of repeating, but for many Agile practitioners it has a slightly different meaning.

For many Agile practitioners, usage of the term 'iteration' refers to the small section of work done in a single 'timebox' and in only 'one repetition'; that is, just doing a small part of the entire work once. So in their Agile terms, there is no idea of doing a piece of work, going back to refine it, then doing it again, say, a third time to 'get it right', which is what you might think 'iteration' means. So, doing the whole job in a series of short 'timeboxes' is what is conveyed by the sense of 'iterative development' by several Agile practitioners.

Just to make sure we are clear on this, although the adjective 'iterative' can be used to describe any repetitive process, it is often applied to any heuristic planning and development process where a desired outcome, like a software application, is created in small sections. These sections are 'iterations'. Each 'iteration' is reviewed and critiqued by the development team and potential end users. Insights gained from the critique of an 'iteration' are used to determine the next development step.

I don't like the idea of using a name in such a misleading fashion. To me, an iteration means testing the first result, going back to revise it and maybe doing that a third time. In 2007, Jeff Patton said:

> I most often see people in Agile development use the term iteration, but really they mean increment. By incremental development, I mean to incrementally add software a time. Each increment adds more software – sorta like adding bricks to a wall. After lots of increments, you've got a big wall. By iterative development I mean that we build something, then evaluate whether it'll work for us, then we make changes to it … We never expected it to be right. If it was, it's a happy accident. Because we don't

expect it to be right, we often build the least we have to to then validate whether it was the right thing to build.[4]

As in our method, we are going with the concept of a development team that includes the product owner, which will greatly help such evaluations. Naturally you must bear in mind what the end product is. Maybe three iterations of building a bridge isn't too good an idea though!

When creating project plans, make time for iterations where appropriate. Don't overstuff plans by scheduling exactly as much work as can be done in a particular time period. A full project plan is a late project. Allow for iterations. Allow for changing and modifying requirements.

Let's take a simple example of iteration. I want to redesign my back garden and I draw, say, three different designs on paper, and discuss them with my wife. If I am lucky (seldom), we will agree on one. More likely the result will be either a hybrid of the three designs. If not, I go back to the drawing board. When we finally agree, I take a piece of string and pegs and mark out the layout of the design on the actual back garden. Now another review. Does it look as good as it did on paper? Again, another possible set of iterations to get it right. So, in our method, iteration is not a single timebox and it can be done from the start of the project, not just during development. Even planning the project can be (and should be) an iterative operation.

2.3.1 Iterating and incrementing

Incrementing means adding a little bit at a time. Here is an example:

---

[4] *www.jpattonassociates.com/dont_know_what_i_want/*.

You open a transport café. Formica tables, metal chairs; one person takes the orders and handles the drinks, another person cooks and serves, (there is a small, basic menu). As business grows, you add more items to the menu, more types of drink, upgrade the chairs, use tablecloths, better signage outside and so on.

2.4 MoSCoW

This is a technique for grading requirements:

M = 'Must have'– this feature is required or the end product may be useless.

S = 'Should have' – a very useful requirement but if not possible, there is a workaround.

C = 'Could have' – a useful feature that would be nice but is not essential.

W = 'Won't have' – a feature that is not needed in this project. It may be added in a later project.

2.5 PRL or prioritised backlog

This is a list of all the work that anyone thinks is required. It may comprise several new requirements, change requests and/or work that was not completed on time and has been returned to the PRL for re-prioritisation against new work. There is no direct PM4A equivalent. It contains all the work (possibly) still to be done, but not in a plan showing when it will be worked on. Work for the next stage is selected from the PRL. The PM4A equivalent to this section is a stage plan.

2.6 Retrospective

This is a regular event that examines how the work processes can be improved based on recent experience. This is the same as PM4A lessons learned. Agile emphasises that it is done more regularly than is implied in PM4A and often feeds back into future work within the project. In PM4A, the use of lessons learned is aimed more at future projects.

2.7 Scrum

Scrum is a working framework within which people can address adaptive problems, while productively and creatively delivering good quality products. It is a way of bringing together the required skills in a team and empowering that team to work in a series of timeboxes to deliver functionality very quickly. In the past, it has been closely aligned with software development, but there are now case studies where it has been used in construction and even emergency aid projects.

I have not used the term 'Scrum' in this generic method of flexible project management, but the philosophy behind the development teams is the same.

2.8 Stand-up meetings (also known as Scrum meetings)

Figure 2.1: Stand-up meetings

Important questions to ask during stand-up meetings:

1. What did you do yesterday?
2. What are you going to do today?
3. What's stopping you from achieving this?

This is a short team meeting, usually held daily and normally lasting 15 minutes or less. The team reviews the previous day's progress in order to plan the next day. This meeting is a course correction, an instance of inspect/adapt for the sake of the work package. The leader of the meeting (the ScrumMaster), has a role to understand any potential blockages and see that they are resolved by the next stand-up (Scrum) meeting.

Together with the information radiator (see chapter 2.2), stand-up meetings dispense with the need for most formal written reports. Because the user (product owner) is part of the team, there is a continuous flow of progress information to the customer.

2.9 Timebox

This is a finite period for work to be carried out to meet an objective or deliver a product. It is a key Agile concept that the time allowed is never extended. Instead, the work allocated is prioritised and done in that order (see MoSCoW). If all the work is not complete by the end of the timebox, the unfinished part is returned to the PRL to be re-prioritised and re-estimated or sized to reflect the remaining effort required.

Timeboxing example:

- Set an objective for a ten-day timebox.
- Load the ten-day timebox with ten days work.
- Then complete the ten days work!
- If you are falling behind schedule, then drop something out of your workload.

The work in the timebox is to deliver the selected features. The PM4A equivalent is a work package with no tolerance on time. The generic method developed in this book will use the term 'work package', but it will follow the Agile timebox rules.

CHAPTER 3: CASE STUDY

Throughout this book, examples will be given using each part of APM. The examples will be based on a case study of a typical 'APM' project. The case study project is as follows:

Case study

The government has announced the introduction of new health and safety regulations affecting hospitals. Although the legislation has not yet been finalised, the government has already announced a date when the legislation will become law. The new rules will affect many of the staff working in hospitals, although the exact number of jobs affected will not be known until the legislation is complete. As time is short, the management of a hospital trust controlling several hospitals in your area, has invited your company, one that specialises in training, to create a training course and to train staff in the new rules. The work includes identifying, by discussion with hospital staff, which staff, procedures and equipment will be affected by the new rules. The project must be flexible and accommodate late changes and additions to the legislation as it passes through the various review groups and changes to the impact that the new rules will have on staff, procedures and equipment.

The project is therefore open-ended, but with a defined end date to ensure compliance with the official start date of the new rules already announced.

In terms of planning, your company has come up with a list of required products and created a project plan for the development of these. These are shown below and explained in chapter 6: Planning.

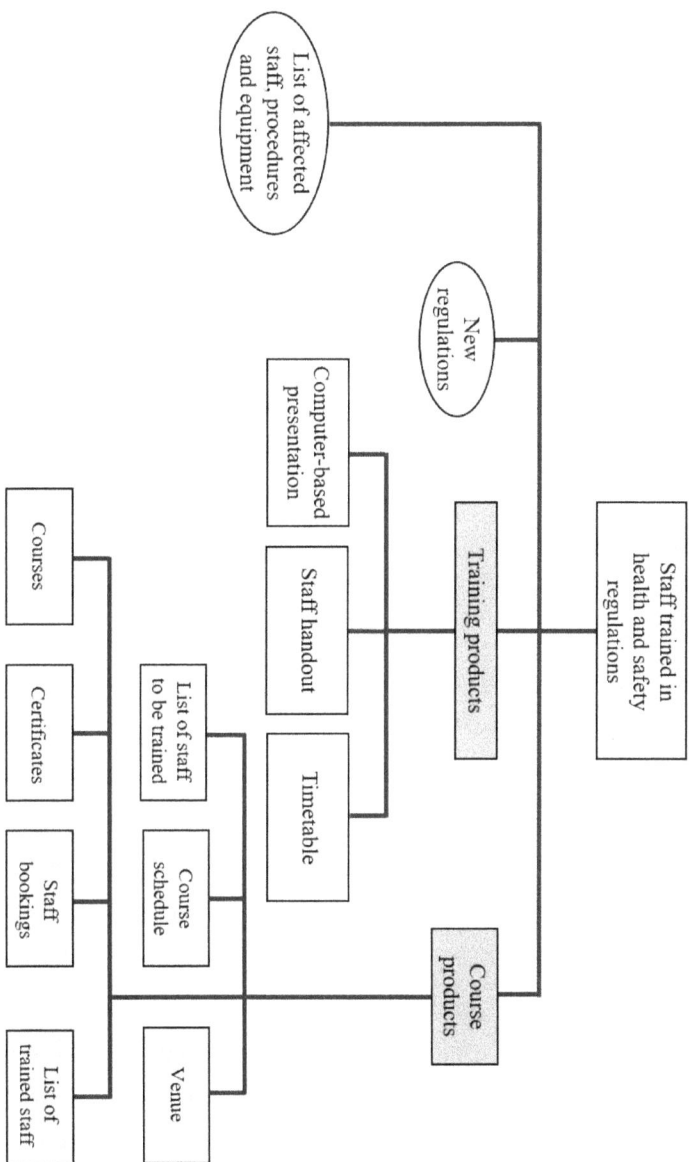

Figure 3.1: Case study list of products

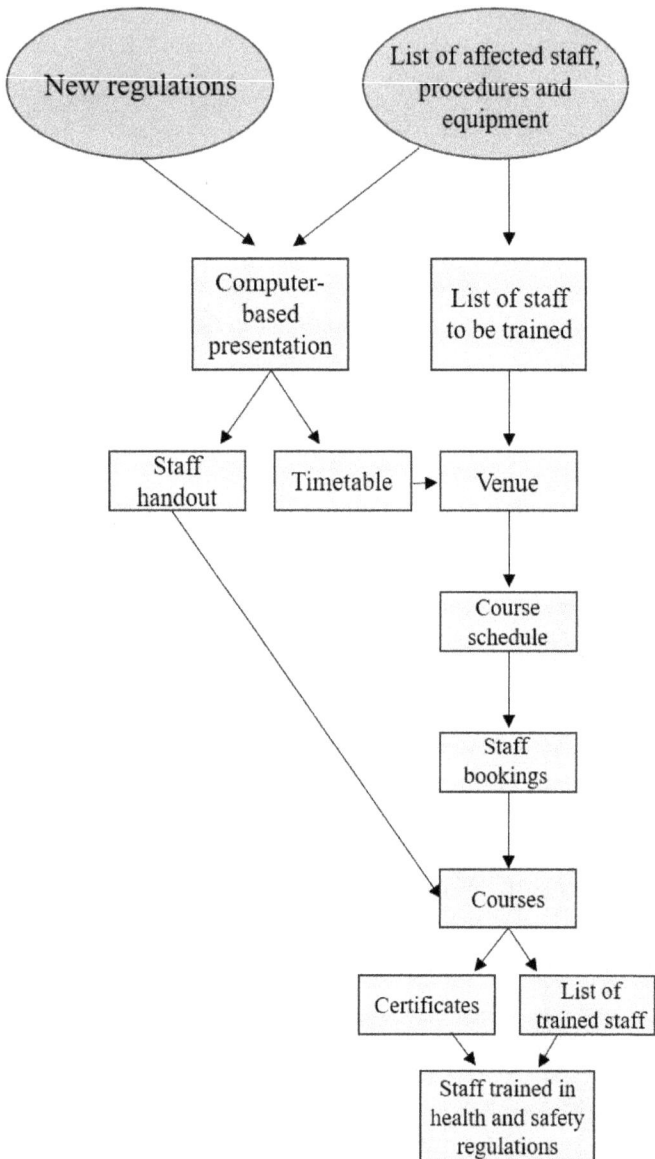

Figure 3.2: Case study project plan

CHAPTER 4: PRINCIPLES

Agile says:

The Agile Manifesto (see section 1.4.1) has 12 principles that can be summed up as[5]:

- Early and frequent delivery of usable products;
- Welcome changes;
- Users and developers working together;
- Self-organising and motivated decision-making work groups;
- Regular reflections on how to improve; and
- Simplicity and excellence.

PM4A says:

PM4A has seven principles:

1. Project justification;
2. Quality;
3. Planning;
4. Project team;
5. Risk;
6. Progress control; and
7. Change.

---

[5] See *https://agilemanifesto.org/principles.html*.

The difference matters because...

On the surface, PM4A focuses on the delivery of a complete solution at the end of the project, whereas regular delivery of usable sub-products and benefits is an essential part of Agile. The APM method needs to embrace regular delivery throughout the project and make this clear.

There is a huge gulf between PM4A's control of changes and Agile's welcome of them until late in development.

PM4A maintains a simple hierarchical structure of roles and decision-making authority, compared to Agile's claim that the teams can make their own decisions. There is very little in Agile about the role of senior management. I believe that the person in charge of the project's finances and who knows company strategy, still needs to manage the project, but the PM4A idea of 'manage by exception' permits a lot of decision-making delegation to teams.

PM4A's organisational structure does not openly encourage a mix of developers and users/product owners in the teams, but this mix does offer great advantages in communication and quick decision-making.

Here is what APM should do:

APM will be based on eight principles:

1. Focus on the business need.
2. Deliver on time.
3. Never compromise on quality.
4. Build incrementally from firm foundations.
5. Develop iteratively.
6. Collaborate.
7. Communicate continuously and clearly.

8. Demonstrate control.

4.1 Focus on the business need

The overriding project goal is to deliver *what the business needs, at the right time and for the right price.* In order to fulfil this principle, APM uses the MoSCoW technique of prioritisation to ensure that the **M**inimum **U**sable **S**ubse**t** to be delivered by the project is clear.

APM incorporates the role of the client, who owns the business case and understands the rationale for the project. The client also understands the user requirements. The development team includes the role of product owner to bring detailed understanding of user needs and to support the communication channel with other users and stakeholders. These roles are more fully explained in chapter 5: Organisation.

4.2 Deliver on time

Delivery on time is often critical for a project. Our method uses time-limited work packages to combine meeting deadlines with a clear focus on business priorities.

4.3 Never compromise on quality

A client may forgive many failings except the delivery of a faulty end product. We establish the client's quality expectations at the beginning, define how that quality is to be achieved and build in quality by constant testing and review.

4.4 Build incrementally from firm foundations

APM advocates building incrementally, starting with the basics. Use just enough analysis and design to create strong foundations and try to deliver business benefits as early as possible.

4.5 Develop iteratively

Start with a high-level statement of requirements and add in the detailed requirements just in advance of building that part of the solution. Each little cycle adds in another level of detail. This allows late changes to be incorporated and the solution detail to evolve as the team learns more about it. User involvement (product owner role) in the development team allows the team to continually confirm that the correct solution is being built.

4.6 Collaborate

For work to be effective, we need a one-team culture of stakeholders and developers. We achieve this by creating a development team that includes all the building skills and knowledge of the user area and empowering the team to take appropriate decisions.

4.7 Communicate continuously and clearly

Many projects fail because of poor communication. APM communicates progress openly via the team composition and an information radiator, and uses modelling and prototyping as a means of demonstrating and selecting solution approaches to the stakeholders.

4.8 Demonstrate control

APM creates a very flexible world of iterating analysis, design, development and discussion. This always requires a strong method of control to be able to demonstrate the current status and ensure rapid agreement to plans without putting the brakes on development. APM also evaluates continuing project justification.

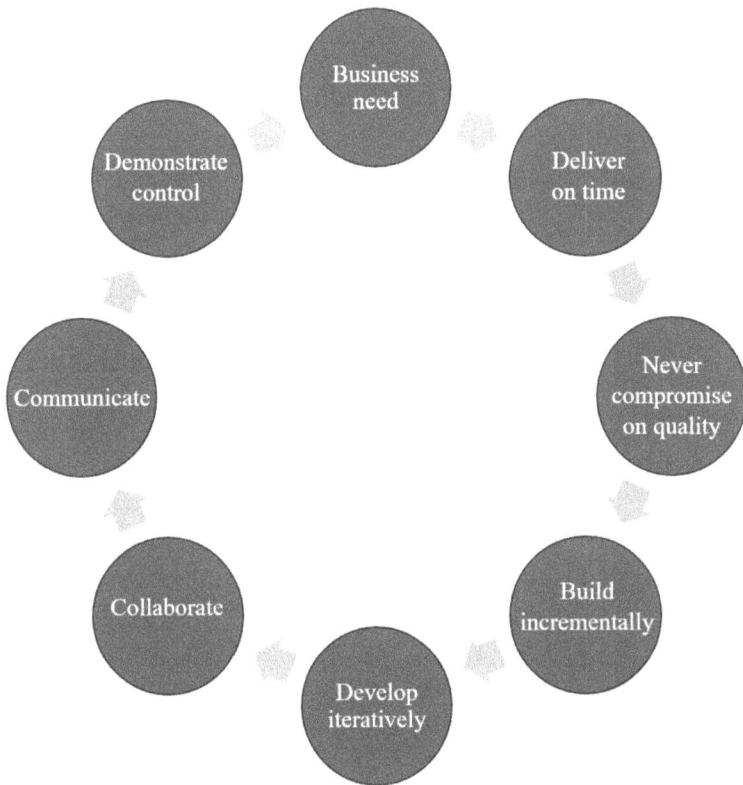

Figure 4.1: The APM principles

Table 4.1: Principles of APM

Project justification	APM emphasises that a viable business case should drive a project. Its existence should be proved before the project is given the initial go-ahead and it should be confirmed at all major decision points during the project. Claimed benefits should be defined in measurable terms so that they can be checked after delivery of the product(s) that achieve that benefit.
Project team	APM defines a structure for the project team – a definition of the roles, responsibilities and relationships of all staff involved in the project. The project team chapter describes roles. According to the size and complexity of a project, these roles may be combined, shared or allocated to an individual.
Quality	APM recognises the importance of quality and incorporates a quality approach to the management and technical processes. It begins by establishing the customer's quality expectations and follows these up by laying down standards and quality inspection methods to be used, and checking that these are being used.
Planning	APM offers plan levels for the size and needs of a project, and an approach to

	planning based on products rather than activities.
Risk	Risk is a major factor to be considered during the life cycle of a project. APM defines the key moments when risks should be reviewed, outlines an approach to the analysis and management of risk and tracks these through all the phases.
Change	Most changes are accommodated within the normal operation of an APM project, but the change chapter also covers the need for the control of any major change that would challenge the current business case or the business's strategy. The chapter is enforced with a change control technique plus identification of the processes that apply the change control. Tracking the key components of a final product and their versions for release is called version control. There are many methods of version control available. APM does not attempt to invent a new one but defines the essential facilities and information requirements for a version control method and how it should link with other APM key chapters and techniques.
Progress	APM provides a small set of controls that enable the provision of key decision-making information, allowing the organisation to pre-empt problems and

make decisions on problem resolution. For the client, controls are based on the concept of 'management by exception', i.e. if we agree a plan, let the team get on with it unless something is forecast to go wrong.

A project is split into phases as an approach to defining the review and commitment points of a project in order to promote sound management control of risk and investment.

CHAPTER 5: ORGANISATION

This chapter supports the principles of collaborate and communicate.

Agile says:

I think this can be summed up in the words of Evan Leybourn, Business Agility Institute, about an Agile structure:

> An organisation that is positioned to adapt to the changing needs of their customers, needs a complementary organisational structure that is both efficient and highly functional. This means a change in the way we think about our organisation. Rather than see the organisation as a pyramid, with executives at the top, graduates and entry level positions at the bottom and everyone else in between; start to think of it has a bee-hive. Hundreds of cells, collaborating towards common goals and outcomes, but ultimately independent in action.[6]

An Agile organisation achieves this by reducing the structural hierarchy and minimising communication overheads through the creation of semi-autonomous, self-organising and cross-functional teams. In this environment, a single, mid-level manager should be capable of supporting 10-20 cross-functional teams, consisting of between 5-9 full-time staff working towards a single, specific outcome.

---

[6] *www.business2community.com/strategy/structure-adaptive-organisation-0733212*.

5: Organisation

To understand what an Agile organisation should look like, there are three concepts you need to comprehend;

1: Cross-functional

Cross-functional teams contain all the key skills required to deliver to the needs of their customers. Unlike traditional hierarchical or matrix management structures, cross-functional teams are responsible for the delivery of a product or service from design to completion, and should not need input from, or handover to, other teams at pre-determined stages.

Benefits to this integration include:

- Faster delivery times by reducing handover and communication delays;
- Consistent ownership of work;
- Rapid response to new issues; and
- Improved information sharing across the organisation.

The best cross-functional teams also integrate the customer, or customer representative, within the team. This will significantly improve customer engagement and, by sharing the accountability for delivery, will dramatically improve the overall outcomes.

2: Self-organising

Self-organising teams have the responsibility and authority to create a functional, internal team structure by replacing, retraining, or reorganising team members as needed. This is most evident when the customer's needs exceed the team's current capabilities. The team should then self-organise by transferring, or in some cases recruiting, staff with those skills into their team.

There are five factors that teams need to take into account to ensure a complementary team structure.

1. Individual Team Members – will have specialisations and preferences, and whilst they should be able to take on different roles, they may not be as productive.
2. Team Members – should be able to take on multiple roles, though they will not be able to take on ALL roles. You will need a good coverage of skills to ensure role coverage.
3. There is a productivity penalty for context switching – you want Team Members to focus on a specific role and switch only as required.
4. Staff who can take on multiple roles – tend to be more creative in their work.
5. The Customer's Requirements – drive the structure of the Team, and often require multiple Team Members in the same role to meet them.

3: Self-managing (or empowered)

But by far the largest bottleneck to organisational agility is the bureaucracy and management needed to ensure that team outcomes align to customer expectations and corporate strategy. In an Agile organisation, this can be overcome by giving individual teams the accountability and authority to engage with, and deliver to, their customers without undue interference within the bounds set by the customers' requirements.

Trust is the most important factor in developing empowered teams. Staff must trust management and management must trust staff. Customers must trust the organisation, and the organisation must trust their customers. Trust comes from communication and respect. Put in place a good communication framework and you are removing many of the impediments to self-management of staff.

A team facilitator may be used to simplify cross-team communication, ensure consensus within a team and align with corporate expectations. Ideally this should be an ordinary team member but may also be a team leader function if required, although it needs to be noted that facilitation and management require different, though complementary, skillsets.

Risks

As with everything, Agile organisational structures and cross-functional teams are not without their risks. For example; understaffed teams may not be able to meet their customer's expectations, a team may lack members with required or specialised skills, or individuals may be unable to dedicate the time required to the team (through either unplanned leave or other corporate requirements). By being aware of these, and related risks, you can put in place simple resource mitigation strategies.

Final thoughts

There are a lot of processes, techniques and frameworks under the Agile umbrella that can be applied outside of ICT (Information and Communications Technology). But, whatever the ultimate goals, an agile organisation emphasises adaptability and customer interaction, but needs to remain aligned to the core Agile values.

PM4A says:

The PM4A principle covering the project team structure is:

- There should be a simple structure of roles that is repeatable for every project;
- Everyone in the team should understand their role and responsibilities, plus those of the other members; and
- Every role should be clear about where the decision-making authority lies.

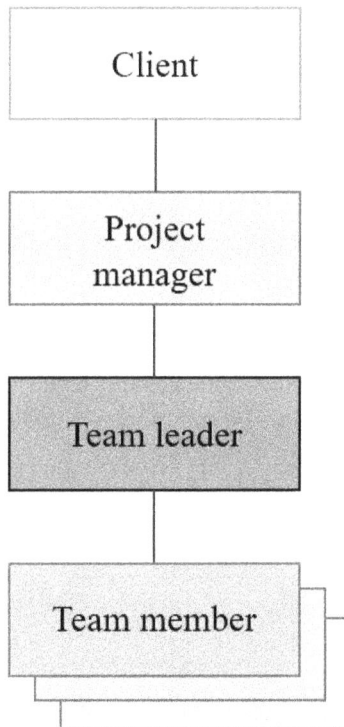

Figure 5.1: The PM4A organisation structure

The difference matters because ...

The PM4A team structure does not show the involvement of the product owner – a major strength of the Agile methods. The PM4A structure is very flexible according to the project size and roles can be combined in several ways, as shown in the figures below.

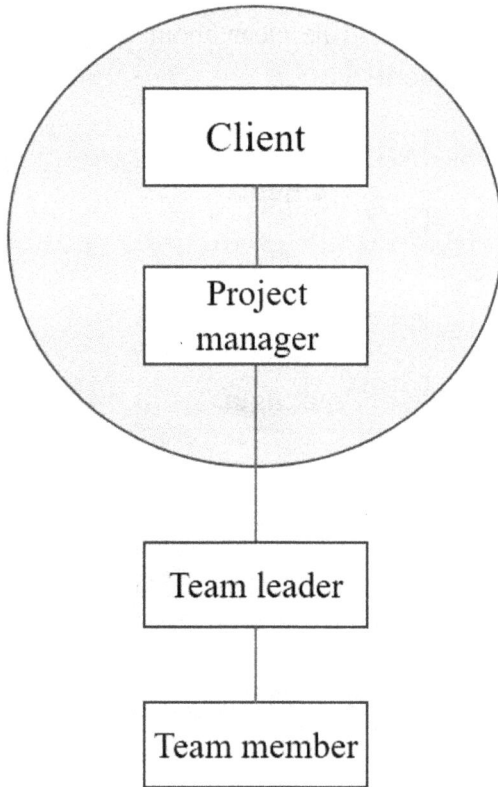

Figure 5.2: Combining the roles of client and project manager

This might be the structure in a small project where the client can also act as project manager.

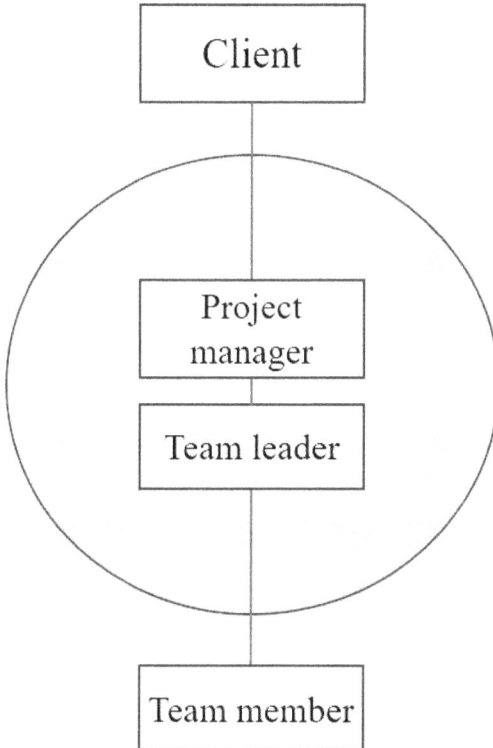

Figure 5.3: Combining the project manager and team leader roles

Again, for small projects it may be sensible to merge the team leader and project manager roles.

These are just two examples combining PM4A roles.

Here is what APM should do:

5.1 Philosophy

Establishing an effective organisational structure for the project is crucial to its success. Every project needs direction, management, control and communication. Before you start any project, you should establish what the project organisation is to be. You need to ask the questions **even if it is a very small project**. Answers to these questions will separate the real decisionmakers from those who have opinions, identify responsibilities and accountability, and establish a structure for communication. Examples of the questions to ask are:

- Who is providing the funds?
- Where is the knowledge of or link to company strategy?
- Who has the authority to say what is needed?
- Who is providing the development resources?
- How will the project be managed on a day-to-day basis?
- How many different sets of specialist skills are needed?
- Who will establish and maintain the required standards?
- Who will safeguard the developed products?
- Who will know where all the documents are?
- Who can authorise changes? Are there to be different levels of this, depending on the impact of the change (change authority)?
- What are the limits to the development team's authority and who sets those limits?

5.2 Overview

APM provides an organisation structure that engages everyone involved: the client, product owner and developer interests. Within the structure there are defined roles and responsibilities for every member of the project management team. The project management team is created when *Proposing* a project and is reviewed as part of the *Plan* phase to see if changes are needed to fulfil the philosophy. The APM organisation structure is shown in Figure 5.4.

APM has an organisation structure that can be tailored to any project. The way in which APM does this is to talk about **roles** that need to be filled, rather than jobs that need to be allocated on a one-to-one basis to individuals. In order to be flexible and meet the needs of different environments and different project sizes, APM's organisation structure define roles that might be allocated to one person, shared with others or combined according to a project's needs.

Corporate or programme management hand the decision making for a project to the client role.

Client

Start-up and initiation team

Development team		
Team lead	Team members	Product owner

Possible assistance from		
Technical expert	Domain expert	Independent tester

Start-up and initiation team		
Team lead	Product owner	Architecture owner

Figure 5.4: The APM organisation structure

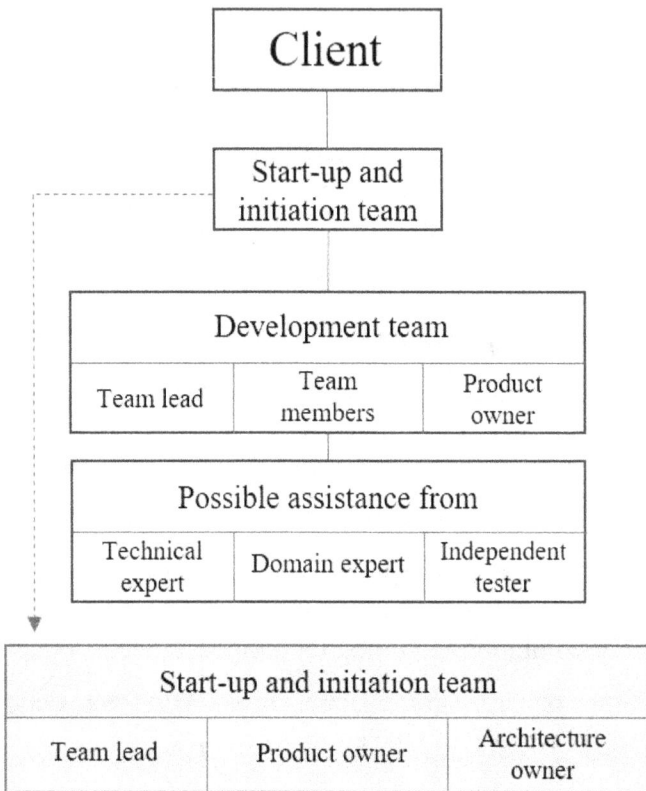

The client is often too busy to look after the project on a day-to-day basis so they delegate to the development team(s), reserving to themselves the key stop/go decisions.

5.3 Corporate/programme management

- Appoint the client.
- Appoint the start-up and initiation team.
- Set any project tolerances of scope and benefits and

document them in the project mandate.

- Provide strategic direction.
- Decide on who can authorise changes.

5.4 Client

The client role is appointed by corporate/programme management to provide overall direction and management of the project. The client is accountable for the success of the project and has responsibility and authority within the limits set by corporate/programme management.

The client must be the ultimate decision-maker with the authority to:

- Approve the project plan;
- Approve stage plans; and
- Commit business resources, such as finance, to the plan.

The role also represents the interests of all those who will use, operate and maintain the final product(s), those for whom the product will achieve an objective or those who will use the product to deliver benefits.

The client is ultimately responsible for the project. They should ensure that the project is value for money, ensuring a cost-conscious approach, balancing the demands of business, user and supplier.

Throughout the project the client 'owns' the project justification and benefits management approach.

The client is responsible for overall business assurance of the project, i.e. that it remains on target to deliver products that will achieve the expected business benefits, and will complete within its agreed budget and schedule. This should include a role of change authority for major changes to the project's specification.

5.5 Start-up and initiation team

The work done by the start-up and initiation team is covered in the *Propose* phase.

This team may be the same team as the development team, but it has specific duties during project start-up and initiation and may require specific skills. It is empowered by the client to identify needs and draw up an outline plan of how to meet those needs.

The roles in this team are team lead, product owner and architect owner. Depending on the project complexity and skills of the team lead, this role may combine with the architect owner.

This team should have the ability to define at a high level what the users need from the project, what type of project approach is selected, how the project will be structured in order to provide these needs and assurance that the project architecture fits in with the environment in which the end product(s) will work.

5.6 Development team(s)

Development teams are made up of three roles: a team lead, a product owner and developers – the number of developers and product owners being flexible according to the amount of work to be done. Development teams should be kept small to avoid communication and control issues.

Development teams are self-organising and choose how best to accomplish their work, rather than being directed by others outside the team. They are cross-functional teams, which should have all the competencies needed to accomplish the work without depending on others who are not part of the team. The development team model is designed to optimise flexibility, creativity and productivity.

The team lead is not so much a project manager as a facilitator and the emphasis in the team is on joint decision making. The presence of a product owner role means that there is always a user representative (at least one – remember the sharing possibility) working with the team to define needs in detail, approve ideas for the provision of features, test and confirm the quality of the developer's work. The product owner also acts as a pipeline with the client on progress and any advice and decisions the product owner feels are needed. The team lead acts as the pipeline to the client in terms of reporting.

The team should provide its own support and version control must be considered. Version control relates to the custody of all master copies of the project's products, and control of the receipt, identification, storage and issue of all project products. Depending on the required formality and need for configuration software, a central specialised function in the company may provide this service to all projects (see chapter 8: Change). Unless a specialised function is to be used, it will often be useful to make the team lead responsible for version control.

5.7 The product owner role

This is an Agile import. It has many benefits:

- Shorter communication lines with users.
- Access to immediate information on what the users want.

- User help in testing.

There are many other benefits. Can the product owner role make decisions and commitments? No one says the role is filled by just one person. Clearly this needs a special type of user to fulfil at least part of the client role, but the possibility is there.

5.8 Stakeholders

In this book we use the term 'stakeholder' several times, so it deserves a fuller explanation. The client clearly has a stake in the success of the project and is therefore a stakeholder. Other stakeholders are individuals or groups who are not part of the project team, but who may need to interact with the project or who may be affected by the project's outcome. They may be supporters of the project or oppose it. Examples include other departments in the company, auditors, shareholders, unions, the general public and government agencies. They will require information from the project, usually progress reports, but occasionally also provide information to the project.

Apart from the client, these stakeholders are not members of the project team. They are not decisionmakers and do not commit resources.

Their information needs are covered in the *Propose* phase.

5.9 APM organisation for large projects

If the project is big enough to require several development teams, you may need to set up teams of the development team roles. For example, a team of all the team leads, a team of all the product owners, etc. These may only be required at the higher level of planning when dividing the forthcoming work between the development teams. These teams may need to communicate with each other to ensure the whole project is heading in the right direction and share useful information. See the proposed structure in Figure 5.5 below.

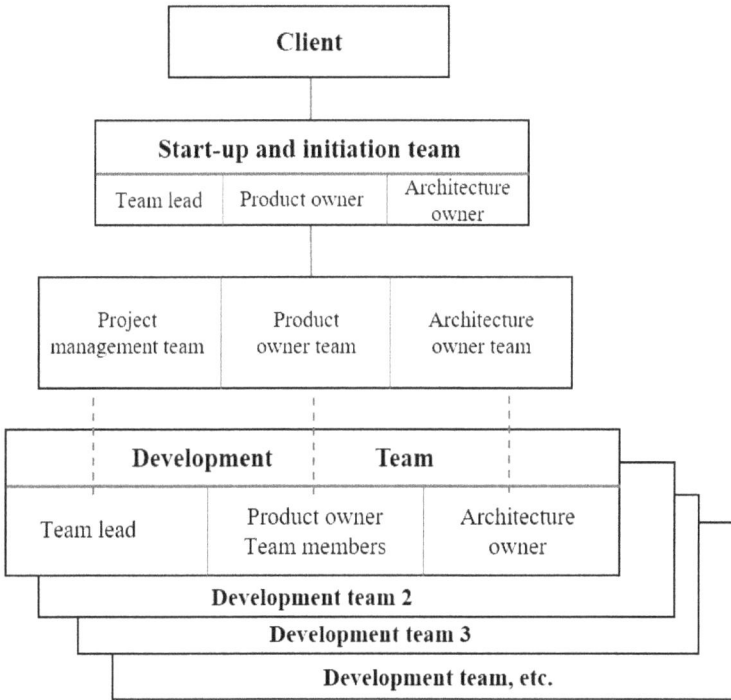

Figure 5.5: The APM organisation structure for large projects

5.10 Case study organisation

For our health and safety case study, the following organisation structure has been agreed.

Case study

The administrator of the hospital trust will be the client. The training company will provide a team lead and two experienced developers. The product owner role will be shared between a senior nurse and head porter, the main staff bodies who will be affected by the new rules. It is not expected that any of the additional optional roles will be required.

CHAPTER 6: PLANNING

Agile's approach to planning

The Agile approach to planning has five steps.

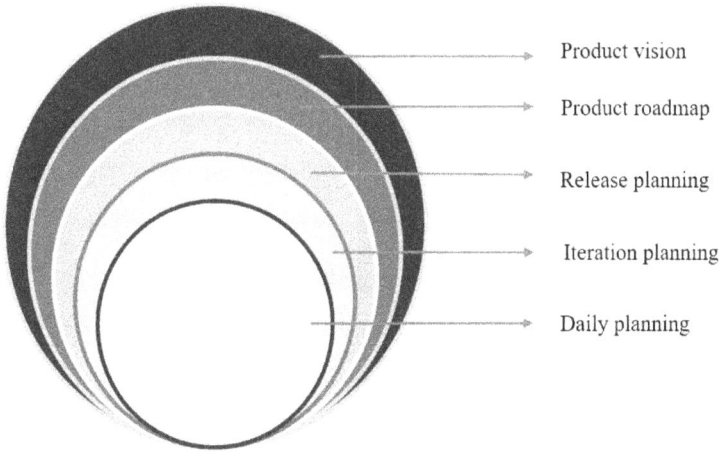

Figure 6.1: Five levels of Agile planning[7]

Be aware that what the article calls 'product backlog', we call the PRL.

1. Product vision

The Agile project life cycle starts with a pre-planning step. This includes collecting and prioritising the major products that are needed, the product backlog.

---

[7] The diagram is based on Koppensteiner, S. & Udo, N. (2009), *An agile guide to the planning processes.*

2. Product roadmap

The team and experts meet and provide high-level estimates for each feature.

3. Release planning

The next step is the planning of releases and iterations (the Agile meaning here of small steps.)

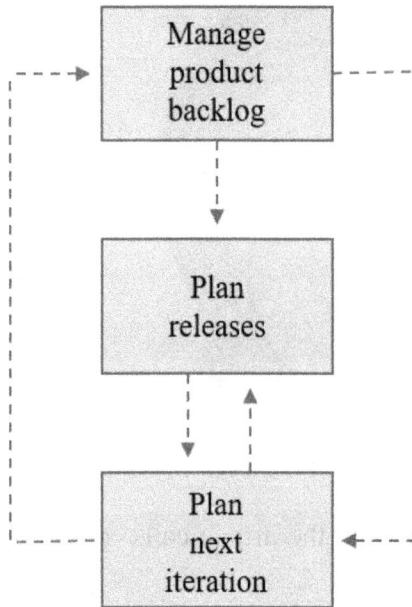

Figure 6.2: Processes for planning of an Agile project (based on Sliger, 2008)[8]

---

[8] Figure 6.2 is based on a PMI diagram from the following article: *www.pmi.org/learning/library/agile-guide-planning-agile-approach-6837*.

4. Iteration planning

The organisation can decide to supply each completed iteration (timeboxed product) to the customer when it becomes available or release a collection of iterations at once in one defined release.

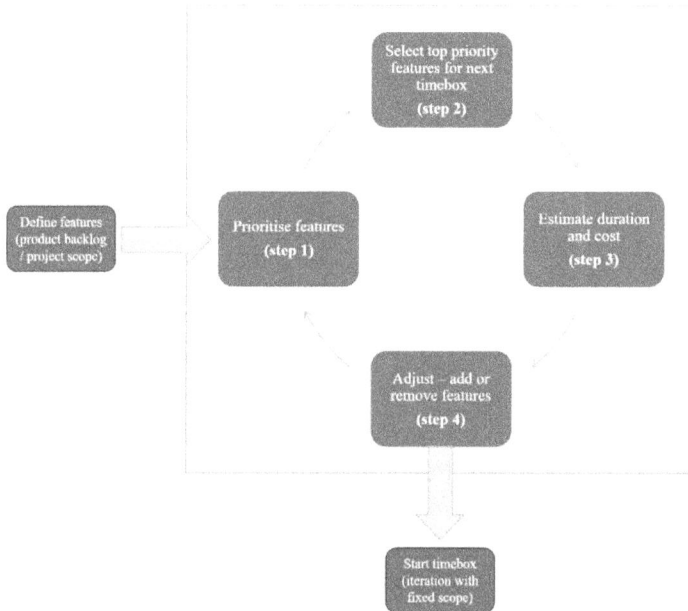

Figure 6.3: Iteration planning[9]

5. Daily planning

As the product backlog can be modified throughout the duration of the project, the number of iterations and releases

---

[9] Figure 6.3 is based on a PMI diagram from the following article: *www.pmi.org/learning/library/agile-guide-planning-agile-approach-6837*.

are subject to change as well. The outcome of iteration and release planning can influence each other. In cases where less (or more) features would be selected during planning of the next iteration, the content and number of future iterations could change. As a result, the collection of iterations assigned to one release could change as well.

PM4A's approach to planning

PM4A creates a project plan in the *Propose* phase. It assumes that the scope of the project and therefore all major requirements are known at the beginning of the project. The project plan must have enough detail to provide cost and duration estimates for the whole project. The business case is built on these figures and the project is expected to stay within these figures (plus any tolerances decided by the client). PM4A planning and control can be said to adhere to a heptagon of parameters, rather than just time, cost and scope (see Figure 6.4). Agile planning almost expects the scope to change as the project progresses but insists that the cost and time boundaries are fixed. Once any PM4A plan is accepted, it becomes a major issue of change control if there is a likelihood of deviating beyond any of the plan's tolerances. Normally there are tolerances on all the parameters of cost, time and scope.

PM4A is really built on completing the development work before one complete handover to the customer.

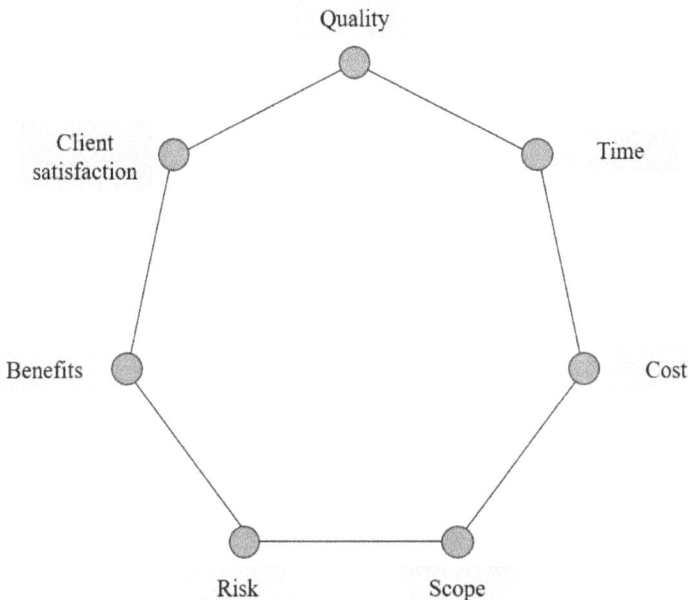

Figure 6.4: The PM4A heptagon

The difference matters because ...

If requirements are not fixed when the project begins, PM4A can suffer considerable wasted time in re-planning and getting client (or even higher management) approval for the revised plan. Agile expects changes to its plans, whereas change is something that PM4A tries to avoid.

Here is what APM should do

6.1 Overview

The purpose of the *Plans* chapter is to define the who, how, when and where required to deliver products in a way that assists control and communication.

The product-based planning technique, described in section 10.3, should be used to create all the plans.

The *Plans* chapter supports the principle of focus on products.

6.2 The APM plan

6.2.1 The Pareto principle

Another motto we should keep in mind as we plan is: 'Deliver something working, sooner rather than later'. This is likely to affect our sequencing of work and delivery in our planning.

> The Pareto principle (also known as the 80/20 rule ...) states that, for many events, roughly 80% of the effects come from 20% of the causes.[10]

For us in a project, it is often the case that proportionately more time is taken to develop areas of the solution that will be used infrequently than to develop the essential functionality. So, let's make a fundamental assumption, the whole solution does not necessarily need to be provided in the first release. As the Pareto principle says, 80% of the solution can probably be produced in 20% of the time that the whole solution would take. If this 80% solution can be released early, business value can be gained from it while work continues on the remaining features. For example, release a version containing only basic, essential error checking and add more complex error responses later.

We learn as we go and allow for detail (and revisions) to emerge later rather than sooner. Hence, we do not attempt to

[10] *https://en.wikipedia.org/wiki/Pareto_principle.*

refine our project plan to too great a detail when we first make it. Requirements are not fully analysed at the outset of the project or at a certain stage, therefore if a requirement does have to be de-scoped, little work has been wasted on it. This de-scoping is always with the agreement of the appropriate stakeholders and has a business-value focus.

6.3 Project plan

The project plan is created during the *Plan* phase.

In APM, the project plan is an overview based on how much information is available at the time. As the basic concept of APM is that not all requirements may be known at the outset and that many changes and additions will come along during the life cycle of the project, the initial project plan may not be the 'finished product'. It is better to make a plan based on what is known at the outset and to make it clear that the project plan will be revised, possibly several times during the project, as more detail becomes clear or changes to user requirements are made.

Early project estimates may be best presented as a range, to indicate the level of confidence in the estimate. The range may show best and worst cases. An estimate should be product-based, although there are other estimating methods, such as algorithmic, analogy, expert judgement, standard ratios, function point analysis and workshops.

Estimating involves forecasting the cost, effort, skills, resource hours and elapsed time to deliver a specific end product. Alternatively, cost, effort, skills and time may be fixed, and the need is to forecast how much functionality can be delivered within these constraints.

Estimating should include:

- Scope;
- Assumptions;
- Dependencies;
- Detail of the calculations made;
- Sources of information;
- Risks; and
- Estimating approach.

If the project is one where it is not known during initiation:

a) If a solution can be found

Or

b) What the best type of solution will be,

then the initial project plan may simply take us up to the point where that exploratory work has been done and the next decision can be made.

The project plan is a mandatory plan. The detailed business case takes the costs of the project from the project plan, and therefore may require an update as the project plan develops.

The project plan will provide a schedule of work, product backlog or list of requirements (PRL) that will feed into the *Create* phase. The client does not want to know about every detailed activity in the project, just a high-level view. This allows the client to know:

- How long the project may take.
- What the major deliverables or products will be.
- Roughly when these will be delivered.
- What people and other resources will have to be

committed in order to meet the plan.

- How control will be exerted.
- How quality will be maintained.
- What risks there are in the selected approach.

The client will control the project using the project plan as a yardstick of progress.

6.4 *Create* phase plan(s)

In order to follow the Agile principle of short 'iterations', it may be necessary to divide the *Create* phase into a series of stages, planning each just before it is to be done. Having produced a PRL and a general guide from the project plan of the sequence in which the requirements need to be built, the development team will select from the PRL the features that should be constructed in the next series of work packages. This should cover a period of one to two months maximum. This will be the next stage and the team should create a plan to do that work. Another part of the philosophy that makes the *Create* phase planning easier is that work is planned shortly before it is due to start, so you have the latest information on actual progress so far available to you.

By configuring each stage plan with the right composition of 'Must have', 'Should have' and 'Could have' requirements throughout the development, the development team will be able to monitor and control the project, adapt if the estimates are wrong and incorporate new requirements as the project progresses without having to take the project over time and budget. If time presses, 'Could have' and then 'Should have' functions can be returned to the PRL for later consideration.

Having created the next stage plan, the project plan should be updated based on the more detailed information from this plan.

6.5 Work package

A work package is a definition of functions or features that are to be delivered in a fixed period, at the end of which the objective has been met and one or more deliverables have been produced. Work packages are a powerful way of keeping the project under control, ensuring that the time deadline is not allowed to slip. In order to achieve this, the stakeholders should agree that if time is threatened, the less important features in the work package, any not vital for that work package deliverable, can be dropped. In Agile this is known as a timebox or iteration.

6.6 Plan checks

The team should consider the following points before approving the plan:

- Plan assumptions;
- Plan prerequisites;
- External dependencies; and
- The MoSCoW grading of requirements.

6.7 The APM approach to planning

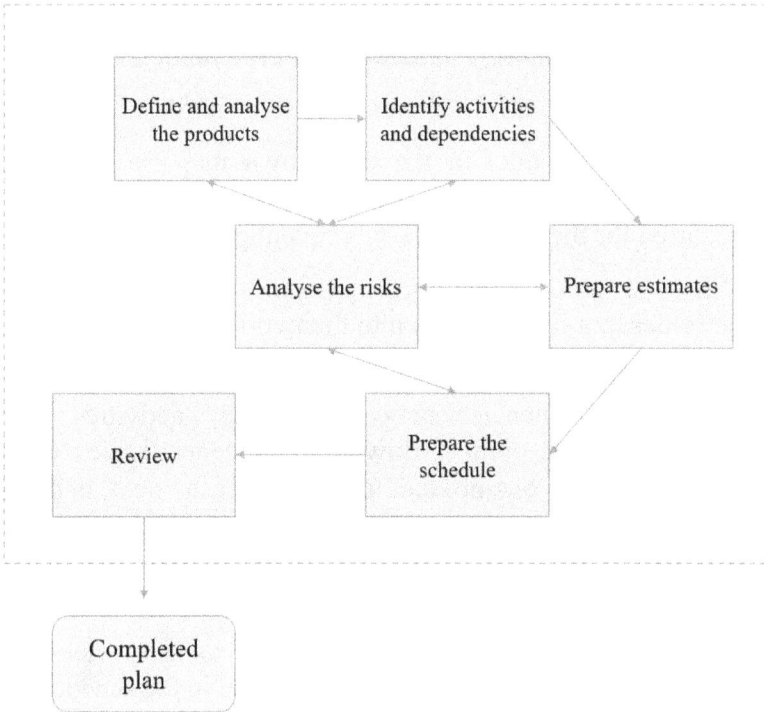

Figure 6.5: The APM planning steps

There are six steps in the APM approach to planning.

6.7.1 Step 1– Define and analyse the products

This step uses the APM technique of product-based planning, which is described in more detail in section 10.3.

- Identify the products required.
- Create a configuration item record for each product.
- Write product descriptions for them.

- Draw a diagram showing the sequence of delivery and dependencies between the products.

6.7.2 Step 2 – Identify activities and dependencies

Note: 'Must haves' should not depend on a 'Should have'.

Break each product in the plan down into the activities needed to produce it. This should continue down to the level required for the work of the subsequent planning activities.

Where a product has been broken down into several activities, put the activities into their correct sequence.

Review the dependencies between products and refine them to give dependencies between the new activities. For example, where product flow diagram dependencies went from the end of one product to the start of the next, is there now an opportunity to overlap, or start some activities on a product before all the activities on the preceding product have been done?

At this point in planning it is possible to use a network planning tool, completion of which will be in the scheduling activity.

6.7.3 Step 3– Prepare estimates

Examine each activity/product and identify what resource types it requires. Apart from human resources, there may be other resources needed, such as equipment or information. With human resources, consider and document what level of skill you are basing the estimate on.

Judge what level of efficiency you will base your estimates on, what allowance you will set for the level of skill available and any non-project time you will need to use.

Estimate the effort needed for each activity/product.

Understand whether that is an estimate of uninterrupted work, or whether the estimate already includes allowances.

Document any assumptions you have made, for example, the use of specific named resources, levels of skill and experience, the availability of user resources when you need them, etc. Check the assumptions with those who have such knowledge, such as the product owner and/or client.

If a network planning tool was used to record the activities and dependencies in the earlier planning activity, this can be completed with the estimates of effort required, allowing the tool to calculate such things as critical path and floats.

6.7.4 Step 4 – Prepare the schedule

Tolerances – cost, time and quality are fixed, and contingency/tolerances come from de-scoping the less-important features. Thus, contingency/tolerance is managed by prioritisation of the features, rather than by adding time or cost tolerances. Contingency is built into estimates and is not an additional percentage of tolerance. 'Must haves' should not account for more than 60% of a work package effort.

- Draw a Gantt chart (see section 6.8 for an example).
- Assess resource availability. This should include dates of availability as well as what the scale of that availability is. Any known information on holidays and training courses should be gathered.
- Allocate activities to resources and produce a draft schedule.
- Revise the draft to remove as many peaks and troughs in

resource usage as possible.

- Add in management and quality activities or products (stage plans only).
- Calculate resource utilisation and costs.

6.7.5 Step 5 – Analyse the risks

- Look for any external dependencies. These always represent one or more risks. What they are providing might not arrive on time. They might be of poor quality or be wrong in some other way.
- Look for any assumptions you have made in the plan, e.g. the resources available to you. Each assumption is a risk.
- Look at each resource in the plan. Is there a risk involved? For example, a new resource doesn't perform at the expected level, or a resource's availability is not achieved.
- Are the tools or technology unproven?
- Take the appropriate risk actions. Where appropriate, revise the plan with resulting countermeasures. Make sure that any new or modified risks are shown in the action log.

6.7.6 Step 6 – Review

- Check the validity of any assumptions made in the plan.
- Check that any prerequisites required by the plan are in place.
- Check that any external dependencies inherent in the plan are reasonable.

- Publish the plan.

6.8 Gantt chart example

Here is a very simple example of a Gantt chart. It shows the activities of a plan against a time frame and allows the user to see clearly the dependencies between the activities.

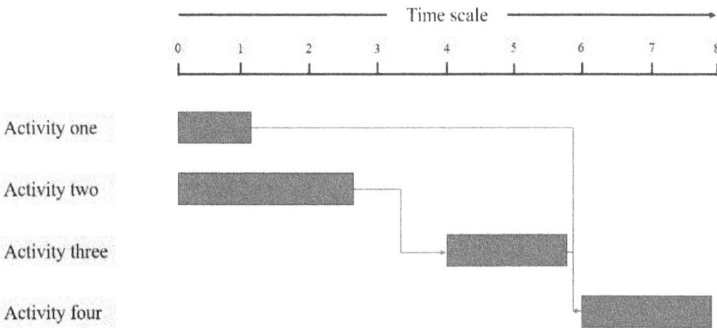

Figure 6.6: Example of a Gantt Chart

Figure 6.6 shows:

- Activities one and two can both begin on day one;
- Activity three cannot begin until activity two is complete; and
- Activities one, two and three must all be complete before activity four can begin.

There is a lot of spare time between the end of activity one and the start of activity four; similarly some spare time between activity two finishing and activity three beginning.

These mean that both activities one and two can be started later, but still finish before their output is required.

The inclusion of the time frame puts dates on start and finish times.

CHAPTER 7: RISK

This is what Agile says

Agile acknowledges risk but doesn't really tackle it. It reflects the fact that Agile-ers are reluctant to consider anything that might get in the way of getting on with development.

Let me quote two statements about Agile and risk management:

- Traditional Risk Management is done up front and tries to envision what could go wrong all the way to the end of the project.[11]
- Agile Risk Management is done more by practices than envisioning. Many Agile practices look to identify and mitigate risk throughout the project.[12]
- Agile exposes and provides the opportunity to recognize and mitigate risk early. Risk mitigation is achieved through: cross-functional teams, sustainable and predictable delivery pace, continuous feedback, and good engineering practices. Transparency at all levels of an enterprise is also key.[13]

These to me are cosy, warm statements, but show two weaknesses:

---

[11] *www.agilealliance.org/wp-content/uploads/2016/01/Agile-Risk-Management-Agile-2012.pdf.*

[12] Ibid.

[13] *www.leadingagile.com/2015/03/agile-is-risk-mitigation.*

1. PM4A and other waterfall methods such as PRINCE2, do not simply consider risk 'up front', but include risk assessment as part of every planning event and monitor risks as an ongoing activity.
2. PM4A offers a comprehensive procedure for the examination of risks and the management of them, Agile does not.

This is what PM4A says

PM4A is very strong on risk management, not only when it should be done, but it also t offers a technique to analyse and manage risks.

The difference matters because ...

Risk is inevitable in changing circumstances and projects are all about creating change, so we need to have a firm hold on how and when to look at risks (and opportunities). Agile doesn't provide this, but PM4A does.

Here is what APM should do

Nothing. We should adopt the PM4A approach to risk assessment and management.

7.1 Philosophy

A risk is an event or combination of events that may or may not occur, but if they do, they will have an effect on achievement of the project's objectives. This means that risk management is a prerequisite to our principle of ***continued project justification.***

- A risk may be a threat or an opportunity.

- Every project is subject to constant change in its business and wider environment. The risk environment is constantly changing too. The project's priorities and relative importance of risks will shift and change. Assumptions about risk must be regularly revisited and reconsidered, for example, at each end phase review.
- The purpose of the risk approach is to identify, assess and control any uncertainties in order to improve the project's chances of success.
- Risk management should be proactive and systematic.

7.2 Risk management strategy

Risks can arise at any time, but there are also defined moments when the risk situation should be examined. A risk management strategy describes the procedures to be used to identify, record, analyse and control risks.

7.2.1 Risk tolerance

Another name for this is 'risk appetite'. An important piece of information is how much risk the client is willing to take in the project. For example, a project to build a new chemical factory would have a very low 'risk appetite', whereas in wartime a project to capture a strategic bridge may have a very high 'risk appetite'.

Risk tolerance can be related to other tolerance parameters; risk to achieving product quality and project scope, and risks to achieving the benefits defined in the project justification.

The organisation's overall tolerance of exposure to risk must also be considered as well as a view of individual risks.

7.2.2 Action log

A project should record risk details in an action log. In APM, the emphasis is on constant visibility of all project information, so the action log should appear as part of the information radiator, possibly with risks grouped as 'high', 'medium' or 'low'.

(Details of the suggested contents of an action log can be found in appendix A.1.)

7.2.3 Risk management times

APM suggests that you:

- **Carry out risk assessments at the start of a project** – make proposals on what should be done about the risks. Get agreement on whether to start the project or not. Risk assessment is done during the *Propose* phase (risks in the project proposal, the project mandate, etc.).

- **Appoint an owner for every risk** – build into the project plan the moments when the owners should be monitoring the risks. Check with the owners that they are doing their job and keeping the risk status up to date.

- **Review every issue for its impact on existing risks or the creation of a new risk** – build the time and cost of any risk avoidance or reduction, for example, into your recommendation on the action to be taken.

- **Review the risks at the end of every phase** – this includes existing risks that might have changed, and new risks caused by the next stage plan (if the project is big enough to use these).

- **Inspect the risks at the end of the project for any that**

might affect the product in its operational life – if there are any, make sure that you notify those charged with looking after the product. (Use the follow-on actions section of the project closure report for this.)

7.2.4 Risk responsibilities

The team has joint responsibility for ensuring that risks are identified, recorded and regularly reviewed. The client has two responsibilities:

1. Notify the team of any external risk exposure to the project; and
2. Make decisions on the team's recommended reactions to risk.

A risk owner should be identified. This is the person best placed to observe and monitor the risk. It might be a member of the team or a member of client management.

7.2.5 Early warning indicators

These are thresholds or levels of items that can be monitored to give advance warning that a risk situation might be developing. Examples are:

- The number of issues being raised;
- The number of quality review errors;
- The amount behind schedule; and
- The amount overspent.

7.3 The risk management procedure

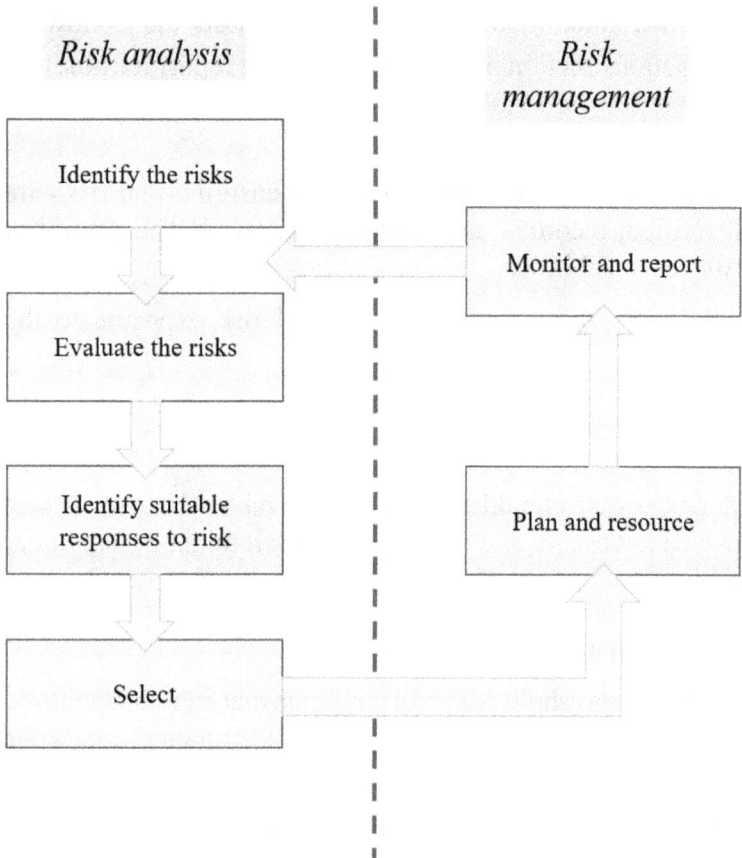

Risk analysis | *Risk management*

Identify the risks

Monitor and report

Evaluate the risks

Identify suitable responses to risk

Plan and resource

Select

Figure 7.1: Risk procedure

The risk procedure has six steps:

1. Identify.
2. Evaluate.
3. Identify suitable responses.

4. Select.
5. Plan and resource.
6. Monitor and report.

7.3.1 Identify

This step identifies the potential risks (or opportunities) facing the project. It is important not to judge the likelihood of a risk at this early stage but to:

- Identify critical parts of the project;
- Note potential sources of risk for these parts;
- Prepare early warning indicators for these;
- Identify risks and record them in the action log; and
- Review captured risks with stakeholders.

7.3.2 Evaluate

Risk evaluation is concerned with the probability, proximity and impact of individual risks, considering any interdependencies or other factors outside the immediate scope under investigation.

Probability

The likelihood of a particular outcome actually happening (including a consideration of the frequency with which the outcome may arise).

Proximity

When considering a risk's probability, another aspect is when the risk might occur. Some risks will be further away in time than others, so attention can be focused on the more immediate ones. This prediction is called the risk's proximity. The proximity of each risk should be included in the action log.

Impact

The effect or result of a particular outcome actually happening. For example, occasional personal computer system failure is fairly likely to happen but would not usually have a major impact on the business. Conversely, loss of power to a building is relatively unlikely to happen but would have an enormous impact on business continuity.

7.3.3 Identify suitable responses

The responses to a risk can be broken down into nine types,

These risk responses can be divided into two categories:

1. Threat
2. Opportunity

Table 7.1: Types of Risk Responses

Avoid (threat)	Terminate the risk – by doing things differently and thus removing the risk, where it is feasible to do so. Countermeasures are put in place that either stop the threat or problem from occurring, or prevent it having any impact on the project or business.
Reduce (threat)	Treat the risk – take action to control it in some way, where the actions either reduce the likelihood of the risk developing or limit the impact on the project to acceptable levels.

Transfer (threat)	This is a specialist form of risk reduction where the financial impact of the risk is passed to a third party via, for example, an insurance policy or penalty clause.
Accept (threat)	Tolerate the risk – perhaps because nothing can be done at a reasonable cost to mitigate it, or the likelihood and impact of the risk occurring is at an acceptable level.
Fallback (threat)	These are actions planned and organised to come into force as and when the risk occurs.
Share (threat or opportunity)	Both parties agree on the likely costs and share any savings or extra costs on either side of this figure.
Exploit (opportunity)	Take action to ensure the opportunity occurs and the positive impact is achieved.
Enhance (opportunity)	Work to improve the chances of the opportunity arising and to enhance the benefits gained from its occurrence.
Reject (opportunity)	A decision not to take the opportunity (at this time) because of other considerations.

If the project is part of a programme, project risks should be examined for any impact on the programme (and vice versa). Where any cross-impact is found, the risk should be added to the other action log.

7.3.4 Select

This involves selection of a risk response from the suitable responses. For each possible action, it is a question of balancing the cost of taking that action against the likelihood and impact of allowing the risk to occur.

The consideration must be done in light of the risk tolerances provided by the client.

It can be useful to look at previous projects' lesson reports to see what risks were considered, what responses were selected and whether the responses were effective.

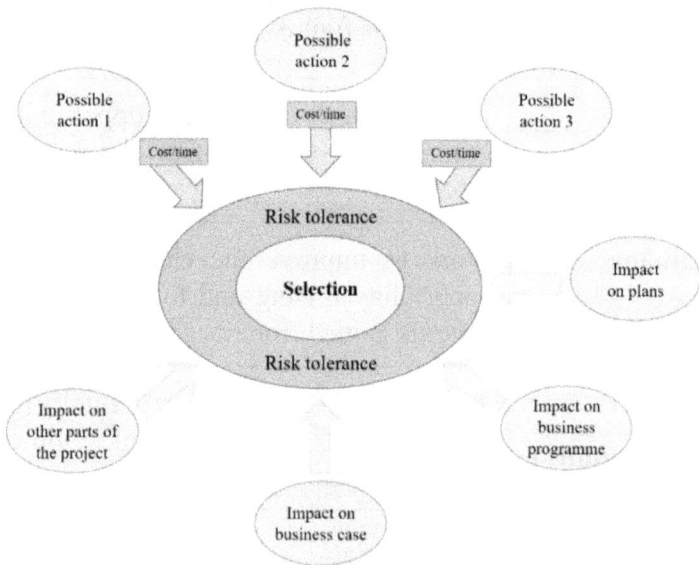

Figure 7.2: Risk action selection

7.3.5 Plan and resource

Having made the selection, implementation will need planning and resourcing, and is likely to include plan changes, new or modified work packages.

A risk 'owner' should be appointed for each risk that requires action. This should be the person with a vested interest in the state of that risk and/or closest to the risk to observe any change to its status.

Results of risk planning are documented in the action log.

7.3.6 Monitor and report

There must be mechanisms in place for monitoring and reporting on the risk actions:

- Some of the actions may only be to monitor the identified risk for signs of a change in their status.
- Risks owned should be reported on the information radiator. Every effort should be made to provide access to all parties. The progress report also summarises the risk status.
- Where a risk actually occurs, an issue should be raised to trigger the necessary actions. There may also be open risks at the end of a project that should be passed to those operating and maintaining the product. This forms part of the follow-on actions, and part of the end project report.
  Consider if there are any risks and corresponding actions that must be noted in the lessons log or the next retrospective meeting.

Table 7.2: Case Study Risk Example

Risk cause	Changes to the legislation.
Event	May occur very late in its passage into law.
Effect	Giving insufficient time to include the changes in the training.
Probability	High.
Proximity	Shortly before the government's announced target date.
Impact	Potentially high.

Table 7.3: What Action Could Be Taken?

Avoid	No – we have no control over when changes may be made or the number of changes.
Reduce	Yes – we should plan to delay printing until the last minute and be ready to lay on extra courses if changes affect staff who we believed were not to be affected. The whole plan should be geared to being ready as early as possible with spare time for late changes.
Transfer	No – We can't just transfer the problem to the hospital trust.

Accept	No – The hospital trust would not be happy if we just accept that our training might not reflect late changes.
Fallback	Yes – This joins with the reduce option in terms of 'if it happens'. As the project will be using APM, it is already geared to accepting changes during development.
Share	No – We don't want to share any costs here.

CHAPTER 8: CHANGE

Agile says:

Agile expects changes and is geared to accept them where they have sufficient impact or benefit, until late in the development cycle.

PM4A says:

PM4A regards change as a problem and builds a big procedure to review them, involving the client in decisions about change.

The difference matters because …

If requirements are not fully known at the outset, a lot of time and effort can be used up by PM4A going through formal procedures. The less well-defined the requirements, the greater the threat of bringing a PM4A project to its knees.

PM4A's *Change* chapter also covers version control, a subject not touched by Agile. Without version control, a project will soon get into serious problems, such as 'Who has what?', 'Are we working on the right version?', 'Why did we create this version?', 'Someone has made a change to this version, but I don't know what it is' and many more.

Here is what APM should do:

APM is designed to start projects and start delivering working products and benefits when the full requirements may still be pretty fluid. We need to move towards the Agile way of easy entry of changes, while having a backstop for changes that are so big in size or impact that they need a decision at client level.

We need to include version control. If APM doesn't do it, something else will have to. You can't just ignore it.

8.1 Philosophy

Change consists of two closely linked activities, change control and version control. Neither can function effectively without the other. Change directly supports the principles of 'focus on products' and 'manage by exception', and indirectly the 'continued project justification' principle.

8.2 Overview of issue and change control

8.2.1 Change control

In any project there will be changes for many reasons:

- Government legislation changes, and this must be reflected in the product specification.
- The users change their mind on what is wanted.
- Because the development cycle is making the product owner think more and more about the product, extra features suggest themselves for inclusion.
- There is a merge of departments, change of responsibility, company merger or takeover that radically alters the project definition.
- A supplier cannot meet an acceptance criterion, such as performance.
- A product delivered by an outside contractor or another project fails to meet its specification.

- All of these need a procedure to control them and their effect on the project. This procedure must make sure they are not ignored, and that nothing is implemented of which the appropriate level of management is unaware. This includes the client.

- An issue is the formal way into a project of any inquiry, complaint or request (outside the scope of a quality review question list). It can be raised by anyone associated with the project. Issues fall into three groups:

  1. A desired new or changed function.
  2. A failure of a product in meeting some aspect of the user requirements or development time limit. In such cases, the report should be accompanied by evidence of the failure and, where appropriate, sufficient material to allow someone to recreate the failure for assessment purposes.
  3. A problem or concern.

  In other words, there is no limit to the content of an issue beyond the fact that it should be about the project.

- Any error found during a quality review normally goes on an action list. There are two exceptions to this:

  1. Where an error is found during quality review that belongs to a different product from the one under review.
  2. Where work to correct an error found during quality review cannot be done during the agreed follow-up period.

Such errors are put onto an issue as a way of getting them into the change control system.

When considering the procedures for handling issues, there is the possibility that the subject will be outside the scope of the project. An example might be a fault in a component that is used in many products across the department or business. Although it is being used in the project, it clearly has a wider implication. There should be a procedure to close the issue off as far as the project is concerned and transfer it to the relevant higher level. The same approach applies if the project is part of a programme and an error is found in a quality review that affects other projects in the programme.

All possible changes should be handled by the same issue and change control procedure. Apart from controlling possible changes, this procedure should provide a formal entry point through which questions or suggestions can also be raised and answered.

8.3 Issue and change control procedure

The procedure has five steps:

1. Capture
2. Examine
3. Propose
4. Decide
5. Implement

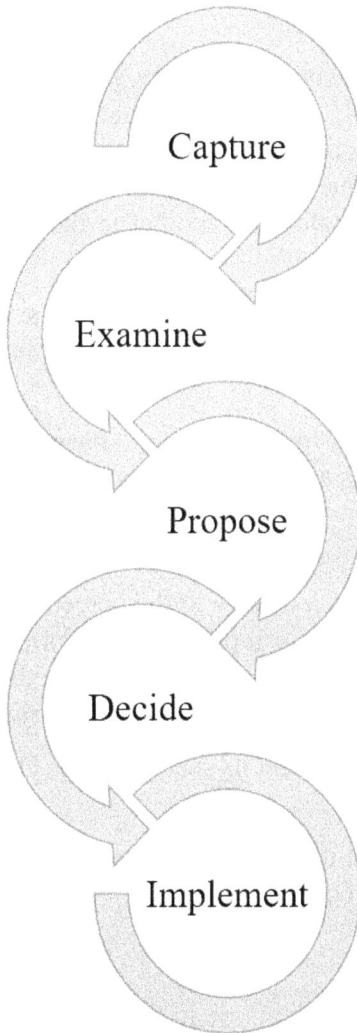

Figure 8.1: Change control steps

8.3.1 Capture

Issues should be handled formally. A project issue should be raised, preferably by the originator, and this should be entered on the action log by the version controller, who will allocate the unique identifier to the issue and pass one copy back to the originator and another to the team. The issue is now classed as 'Open'.

The first step is to carry out a brief analysis, just enough to decide what type of issue it is. The outcome is normally one of the following:

The issue is proposing a change to a **baselined** configuration item. The issue is a **request for change** and the decision can only be made by the client (or change authority if one has been appointed).

The issue requests a change to the agreed user specification, acceptance criterion or a product description. The issue is a **request for change** and should be added to the PRL for prioritisation with the other remaining work.

A product does not meet its specification. The issue is an **off-specification.**

The issue asks a question or voices a **concern** but will not lead to a product change.

8.3.2 Examine

The team allocates the issue to the person or persons on the development team best suited to perform a full impact analysis. The issues are evaluated in terms of their impact on:

- Time;
- Cost;
- Quality;

- Scope;
- Benefits; or
- Risks.

The aim is to make recommendations on their resolution. The analysis should cover all aspects, business, user and supplier.

If the request is a change to a current work package, it can be discussed by the team at the next stand-up meeting to decide if it should be added to the current work package or sent to the PRL.

All project issues must be closed by the end of the project or transferred to follow-on actions, part of the end project report. The transfer of an issue to these recommendations can only be done with the approval of the client.

8.3.2.1 Request for change

A request for change records a proposed modification to the user requirements.

The request for change requires analysis to see how much work is involved. The version control records hold information that will help to identify what other products will be affected.

It is particularly important that any **baselined** products that will need to change are identified because the client has already been told of the completion of those items. The client must therefore approve any change to such items.

8.3.2.2 Off--specification

An off-specification is used to document any situation where the product is failing to meet its specification in some respect.

The next unique issue identifier from the register is allocated and a copy of the issue is sent to its author. Development team members carry out an impact analysis to discover which products are affected by the off-specification. They then assess the effort needed.

8.3.3 Propose

With the results of the impact analysis available, the next step is to look at alternative actions and propose the best response.

In APM, the best response is noted on the project issue. A decision is made on whether the change can be made within the current work package. If not, the issue is added to the PRL, where it will take its turn in the next re-prioritisation of requirements.

To help in the prioritisation of an issue, it should be awarded a priority rating based on MoSCoW. This can be one of four:

- Must have.
- Should have.
- Could have.
- Won't have.

8.3.4 Decide

8.3.4.1 Request for change

For the request for change to be implemented, it must be approved by the appropriate level in the severity table. Whose decision it is will be documented in the change control approach.

The decision must be made by the client if the change is to one or more configuration items that the client has already been told are complete (to any baseline, not necessarily the final one). More than anything, this is to retain the client's confidence level. If the client has been told that something is finished and later finds out that it has been changed without consultation, their sense of being in control evaporates. The matter is referred to the client by means of a problem report (see appendix A.4).

The client is the key role in any request to implement any major changes. All those requests for change that have not been decided by the development team are passed to the client. It should be the client's job to put them in order of priority for a decision.

The client's decision may be to:

- Implement the change;
- Delay the change to an enhancement project after the current one is finished;
- Defer a decision until a later meeting;
- Ask for more information; or
- Cancel the request.

If the client has delegated the responsibility for a decision on problem reports to the development team, then the team will play the role described above. The decision should be documented on the problem report and in the action log.

Whenever its status changes, a copy of the issue report should be sent to the originator.

8.3.4.2 Off-specification

As with requests for change, the decision on action is taken by either the development team or the client. If the error is because of a failure within the development team's responsibility, the onus is on the team to correct the problem within the work package. If this cannot be done, rather than extend the allowed time for the work package, lower-level requirements should be omitted and returned to the PRL for future consideration.

If the off-specification requires changes to one or more configuration items that the client has already been told are complete (to any baseline, not necessarily the final one), the client must make the decision based on a problem report.

The client's decision may be to:

- Correct the fault – this means putting the issue on the PRL;
- Delay correction of the fault to an enhancement project after the current one is finished;
- Defer a decision until a later meeting; or
- Ask for more information.

The decision should be documented on the problem report and the action log, and an updated copy filed. Whenever its status changes, a copy should be sent to the originator.

8.3.5 Implement

The development team is responsible for scheduling any approved changes. This work will possibly involve the issue of a new version of one or more products by the version controller.

On receipt of a completed request for change or off-specification, the version controller should ensure that any amended products have been re-submitted to the configuration library. The finalised request should be stored and the originator advised. The action log should be updated with the final details and the originator advised.

8.4 Version control overview

If your project creates or changes more than one product, or you have more than one person working on the same or different versions of the same product, then you already are dealing with some form of version control. It's just a question of whether you are doing it in a controlled manner and can track what's going on.

No organisation can be fully efficient or effective unless it manages its assets, particularly if the assets are vital to the running of the organisation's business. A project's assets likewise must be managed. The assets of the project are the products that it develops.

Within the context of project management, the purpose of version control is to identify, track and protect the project's products as they are developed.

In APM, the norm is for someone in the development team to do the version control job in addition to their normal work. It is better to have one person responsible, rather than attempt to share this work.

The objective of version control is to achieve a controlled and traceable product evolution through properly authorised specifications, design, development and testing.

This objective is met by defining and ensuring:

- The issue and control of properly authorised specifications;
- The issue and control of properly authorised design documents;
- The issue and control of properly authorised changes to the specification or design documents; and
- The control of the various versions of a product and their relationship with its current state.

Version control is also the process of managing change to the elements that comprise a product. It implies that any version of the product and any revision of the chapters that make up the product can be retrieved at any time, and that the resulting product will always be built in an identical manner. Product enhancements and special variants (such as foreign language documentation) create the need to control multiple versions and releases of the product. All these must be handled by version control.

Version control is a discipline that:

- Records what components or products are required in order to build a product;
- Provides identifiers and version numbers to all products;
- Controls access and change to components of a product once they have been declared complete by the developer;
- Provides information on the impact of possible changes;
- Keeps information on the links between the various parts of a product, for example, what items comprise a product, where is component X used, or what does the 'full product' consist of;

- Provides information on the status of products (configuration items) being developed, including who is responsible for the development;
- Is the sensible storage place for product descriptions; and
- Gives a project team the assurance that products are being developed in the correct sequence.

Version control holds a central position in project work. Product breakdown structures used in planning provide the identification information for the configuration items. The links allow the construction of the product flow diagrams. They offer input and verification of the products required for a plan. You cannot adequately do change control without version control. It provides product copies and product descriptions for quality checks and keeps track of the status of the product. It provides the information to construct a release package, either a complete one or a partial one, and then records the issue of a release.

Version control records are valuable assets in themselves. Version control helps a business know what its assets are supposed to be, who is responsible for their safekeeping and whether the actual inventory matches the official one.

Version control gives control over the versions of products in use, identifies products affected by any problems and makes it easier to assess the impact of changes.

Version control supports the production of information on problem trends, such as which products are being changed regularly or frequently, thereby assisting in the proactive prevention of problems.

Where the end product is to be used in more than one place, version control helps organisations to control the distribution of changes to these operational sites. Where there is any volume of changes, there will be the need to decide between putting together a 'release package' of several changes or issuing a complete new product. The latter may be a more controlled and cost-effective means of updating an operational product than sending out one changed product at a time. The decision and control mechanisms for this are part of version control.

Version control supports the maintenance of information on proven reliable releases to which products can revert in case of problems.

Because all products are under the control of version control once they have been developed, it makes it more difficult for them to be changed maliciously, thus improving security.

The data held in the version control library helps to recreate a release after any disaster by identifying the products required and their storage place.

8.4.1 Version control detail

Version control covers all the technical products of a project. It should also be used to record and store management and quality products, such as plans, quality check details and approvals to proceed.

8.4.1.1 Costs

There are the expected costs of training a team member in version control. There may be a central office (say part of a central project support office) that provides version control functions to several projects. If so, liaison must be set up to work with this role.

It is very difficult to keep the comprehensive records required to do a complete job of version control in a medium to large project without a computer database and software. The costs here are far outweighed by the increase in speed, capacity and detail of information. The increase in speed of reaction by the version controller probably reduces the number of version controllers needed to cover all the site's products.

The need to go through the version control tasks may slow down slightly the handover of a finished item or the implementation of a change. However, this penalty is very small when weighed against the risk and impact of operationally using a product that is from an incorrect release or has not been checked out. Without it there is also the risk of more than one person changing a product simultaneously, resulting in all but the final change being lost.

8.4.1.2 Possible problems

If products are defined at too low a level, the version controller may be overwhelmed by the amount of data to be fed into the library. This is a particular problem when no version control software is being used.

If products are defined at too high a level, the information for impact analysis may be too vague and result in a larger than necessary product change being indicated, e.g. altering a whole set of sub-products when only one sub-product is affected.

Procedures must cater for emergency changes, where an emergency change is required in order to let the operational product continue.

Where version control is new, development staff may be tempted to view its controls as bottlenecks and bureaucracy. However, it has been used in engineering for many years and is regarded in those circles as essential. It is also regarded as an essential part of any quality product, should you be looking for accreditation under such standards as ISO 9001. It is regarded as essential because of the control it gives and experience over many years, which has shown its value and the cost of problems arising when it is not used.

8.4.1.3 When is it done?

A version control approach is required as part of the *Propose* phase. This should state:

- What method is to be used;
- Who has the responsibility for version control;
- What naming convention will be used to identify products of this project;
- What types of product are to be covered; and
- What types of status are to be used (e.g. 'allocated', 'draft available', 'quality checked')?

Once a product has been identified as required, it should receive an identifier from the version control method. Sensibly, this should coincide with the creation of a draft product description.

Among the version control planning activities required are those to identify what **baselines** will be required (baselines are explained later in this chapter) and for what purpose, which baselines exist concurrently, and which cannot, and when baselines will be taken.

The status of a product should be tracked from the moment the product description is created.

8.4.1.4 Version control records

The detail to be kept about the products will depend to some extent on the complexity of the end product, the number of products, the resources available to keep the records and the information demanded by the maintenance and support groups. Table 8.1 shows a list of potential information about a product that should be considered against the needs of the project.

It should be noted that the first three pieces of information uniquely identify the configuration item.

Table 8.1: Assessing the Needs of the Project

Project identifier	A unique identifier allocated by either the version control software or the version controller to identify all products of the project.
Item identifier	Unique identifier for a single product.
Current version number	The number of this version of the product. This is usually linked to a baseline. You may wish to divide this into version and sub version number, e.g. 3.1.
Variant	(If required) covers, for example, the product in a different language, such as a user manual.

Item title	Same as the name in the product breakdown structure.
Date of last status change	The date of the last status change.
Item attributes	You may wish to differentiate between management and specialist products, for example, or separate the specialist products into groups, such as those provided from an external source.
Stage	The stage during which the product will be created or obtained and used.
Owner	Who owns and is responsible for any decisions to alter it. This may be different to the person working on the product.
Users	The person or group(s) who will use the product.
Presenter	The person or team responsible for creating or obtaining the product.
Date allocated	The date allocated for work.
Location	Where the product is kept.
Source	The name of the supplier if from an external source.

Links to related products	Products of which this product forms a part.
Status	Current status of the configuration item as defined in the approach – you might have your own ideas on the possible entries for this, but the following list may give you some extra ideas:

For the Status row, the following list appears:

- Product not defined.
- Product description in progress.
- Product description written.
- Product description approved.
- Product ordered.
- Product in progress.
- Draft version available.
- Product in test.
- Product under review.
- Product approved.
- Product accepted.
- Product delivered.
- Product installed.
- Product under change.

(Not all of these need to be used, just those that fit your status needs.)

Copy holders and potential users	Details of who holds a copy of the product plus who may require a copy when the product reaches a certain status.
Project issue cross reference	If this version of the product has been caused by an issue, this should be cross-referenced as an audit trail.
Correspondence cross reference	A reference to any relevant correspondence that affects this product or version of it.

8.4.1.5 Baselines

Baselines are moments in a product's evolution when it and all its components have reached an acceptable state, such that they can be 'frozen' and used as a base for the next step. The next step may be to release the product to the customer, or it may be that you have 'frozen' a design and will now construct the products.

Products constantly evolve and are subject to change as a project moves through its life cycle and, later, in the operational life of the product. A development team will need to know the answer to many questions, such as:

- What is the latest agreed level of specification to which we are working?
- What exact design are we implementing?
- What did we release to site X last January?

In other words, a baseline is a frozen picture of what products and what versions of them constituted a certain situation. A baseline may be defined as a set of known and agreed configuration items under change control from which further progress can be charted. This description indicates that you will only baseline products that represent either the entire product or at least a significant product.

A baseline is created for one of several reasons:

- To provide a sound base for future work.
- As a point to which you can retreat if development goes wrong.
- As an indication of the component and version numbers of a release.
- As a bill of material showing the variants released to a specific site.
- To copy the products and documentation at the current baseline to all remote sites.
- To represent a standard configuration (e.g. product description) against which supplies can be obtained (e.g. purchase of personal computers for a group).
- To indicate the state the product must reach before it can be released or upgraded.
- As a comparison of one baseline against another in terms of the products contained and their versions.
- To transfer configuration items to another library, e.g. from development to production, from the supplier to the customer at the end of the project.

The baseline record itself should be a product so that it can be controlled in the same way as other products. It is a baseline identifier, date, reason and list of all the products and their version numbers that comprise that baseline. Because of its different format it is often held in a separate file.

8.4.1.6 Version auditing

Version auditing checks whether the recorded description of products matches their physical representation and whether items have been built to specification. There are two purposes of version auditing. The first is to confirm that the version control records match reality. In other words, if my version control record shows that we are developing version 3 of a product, I want to be sure that the developer has not moved on to version 5 without my knowing and without any linking documentation to say why versions 4 and 5 have been created. The second purpose is to account for any differences between a delivered product and its original agreed specification. In other words, can the version control records trace a path from the original specification through any approved changes to what a product looks like now? These audits should verify that:

- All authorised versions of items exist;
- Only authorised items exist;
- All change records and release records have been properly authorised by the development team; and
- Implemented changes are as authorised.

Version auditing is defined as an inspection of the recorded version control description and the current representation of that item to ensure that the latter matches its current specification. The inspection also checks that the specification of each item is consistent with that of its parent in the structure. In a sense, it can be regarded as similar to stock control. Does the book description match with what we have on the shelf? In addition, the audit should ensure that documentation is complete and that project standards have been met.

In engineering establishments, the aim of version auditing is to check that, in spite of changes that may have taken place in requirements and design, the items produced conform to the latest agreed specification and that quality review procedures have been performed satisfactorily. This verifies at successive baselines that the item produced at each baseline conforms to the specification produced for it in the previous baseline, plus any approved changes does this.

Version audits should be done:

- Shortly after implementation of a new version control system;
- Before and after major changes to the structure of the project's end product;
- After disasters, such as the loss of records;
- On detection of any 'rash' of unauthorised products; and
- Randomly.

8.4.1.7 Version audit checklist

Here is an example audit checklist. The following items should be examined:

- Do the version records match the physical items?
- Are (randomly tested) approved changes recorded in the action log? Are they linked to the appropriate products? Is their implementation controlled by the version control method?

- Does the version library accurately reflect the inclusion of any random products? Are there links to relevant project issues?
- Are regular version audits carried out? Are the results recorded? Have follow-on actions been performed?
- Are (randomly tested) archived and backup versions of products retained and recorded in the correct manner?
- Are the recorded versions of products used in multiple locations correct?
- Do product names and version numbers meet naming conventions?
- Is version library housekeeping carried out in accordance with defined procedures?
- Are staff adequately trained?
- Can baselines be easily and accurately created, re-created and used?

8.5 Links

There is a very strong link between change control and version control. They are inseparable. You can't have one without the other. It is sensible to give the same person or group responsibility for both elements.

Version control links to quality. If you lose control over which versions should be used, release old versions of components or allow the release of an untested change, the quality of the product will suffer.

8.6 Dos and don'ts

- Do relate the complexity of the version control method to the needs of the project.

- Don't underestimate the importance of version control. As said at the beginning of the chapter, if there is more than one person working on the project, if there will be more than one version of a product, you need version control. Make sure it is adequate for the job.

- Do think about the stability of the customer's specification before you dive into a project. The less stable it is, the more change control will be required and the higher the cost of authorised change is likely to be.

- Don't underestimate the importance of change control. There is no project control without it.

8.7 If it's a large project

APM is intended to accommodate changes smoothly and until late in the development cycle. Any change requests are noted on a project issue and added to the PRL for prioritisation. In the *Plan* phase there is a point where the client is asked if they wish to put any limit on the size of change that can be allowed without reference to the board.

8.8 If it's a small project

Members of the team can probably do version control. I looked at a feasibility study where one of the analysts performed the version controller's job. It took about two hours each week. There was a lockable filing cabinet in which the various versions of sections of the report were kept. Team members were responsible for telling the version controller when they wanted to move to a new version. The version controller checked the log and allocated the next version number, having first logged the reason for the change, i.e. a reference to the issue. These reasons had to be documented. Once a fortnight the analyst would take the configuration records round the office and check that there was a match between the records and the version numbers being used (version audit).

Change control will still be important.

CHAPTER 9: PROGRESS

Agile says:

The following summary comes from Rick Freedman, writing in *Tech Decision Maker*, 19 July 2010:

> Using Scrum as an example, the reporting expectations are clearly defined; different agile methods have different standards. In Scrum, we typically create four reports at the end of each iteration:
>
> - the Product Backlog, which lists all the features that make up the entire product
> - the Sprint Backlog, which include the features we've committed to deliver in the next iteration
> - the Changes report, which details the differences between the Product Backlog and the Sprint Backlog
> - the Burndown report or chart, which illustrates (usually in the form of a trend graph) the work we've actually "burned through," giving us a real-world view of the team's progress.[14]

PM4A says:

PM4A is very strong on reporting progress, issues and risk situations. Just look at the templates available to disseminate information in a standard format. Templates are a good memory jogger to ensure that the creator doesn't forget some vital piece of information. I think it is good for a reader to

---

[14] *www.techrepublic.com/blog/tech-decision-maker/agile-reporting-methods-for-project-managers/*.

know what information to expect and where in the document to find it. PM4A templates:

- Action log.
- Daily log.
- Problem report.
- Progress report.
- Project closure report.
- Project issue.
- Risk report.
- Work package.

Apart from these templates, just think of the wealth of information in other PM4A document templates:

- Post project review plan.
- Product description.
- Product version control.
- Project justification.
- Project mandate.
- Project proposal.

In the wrong hands, reporting can be turned into a monster that devours time that should be better spent on development or control. However, I am sure we all agree that communication is vital in a project, and from experience I would rather not leave this to individual choice.

The difference matters because ...

No project manager, Agile or traditional, denies that stakeholders deserve visibility into the project for which they are paying and on which they are relying for added business value. Any disagreement is one of degree and focus.

Agile focuses on defining progress by the products and benefits delivered. This matches the development cycle and the less time-consuming and formal we can make it, the better.

Here is what APM should do

PM4A should adopt the concept of short meetings and progress visibility by what has been delivered with this information being visible to all and kept up to date.

9.1 Introduction

The *Progress Control* chapter supports the principles of management by exception, management by phases and continued project justification.

Project control is perhaps the key element in project management. Some would say that risk management is the cornerstone of project management, but, although I deal with risk management in its own chapter, I see it as one part of control. Whatever your opinion is, I think we can all agree it is vital.

9.2 Project proposal and plan

However large or small the project, it is sensible to begin a project with a *Propose* and a *Plan* phase. This is where the client and start-up team decide if there is agreement on:

- What the project is to achieve;

- Why it is being undertaken;
- How and when the required products will be delivered; and
- How the project will be monitored and controlled.

This information is documented in the project justification, which is then 'frozen' and used by the client as a benchmark throughout the project and at the end to check performance and deliverables.

9.3 Project plan

The project plan shows the stages and their expected timeframes, based on the priorities known at the time. It will be regularly updated as deliveries are made, giving similar information to the Agile burndown chart.

9.4 PRL

This is like the product backlog in Agile. It will normally consist of a one-line description, allocated priority and status, for example, 'unallocated', 'done', 'part of stage/work package x'.

9.5 Stages

If the project size warrants it, the *Create* phase may be broken down into a series of stages. A stage is a collection of activities and deliverables whose delivery is managed as a unit. The equivalent in Agile is a sprint backlog. As such, it is a sub-set of the project, and it is the element of work that the development team is managing on behalf of the client at any one time.

Stage-limited commitment

At the end of each stage the client only approves a detailed plan to produce the products of the next stage. The project plan is updated, but this is for the guidance of the client mainly and will become more accurate as more stages are completed.

The reason for breaking the *Create* phase into stages is to give the client opportunities for conscious decision making as to whether to continue with the project or not, based upon:

- A formal analysis of how the project is performing, based on information about results of the current stage.
- An assessment of the next stage plan.
- A check on what impact the next stage plan will have on the overall project plan.
- A check to confirm that the project justification is still valid.
- Confirmation that the risks facing the project are manageable.

In theory, at the end of each stage the client can call for cancellation of the project because of the existence of one or more possibly critical situations. For example, the organisation's business needs may have changed to the point at which the project is no longer cost-effective.

9.6 Tolerance

Tolerance is the permissible deviation above and below the planned target for time, cost, quality, scope, benefits and risk without escalating the deviation to the next level of management. Different amounts of tolerance can be applied at project, stage and work package levels.

In our method there is no tolerance on time, budget or quality. Cost, time and quality are fixed. Contingency/tolerances come mainly from de-scoping the less-important features, although there may be tolerances for risk and benefits, for example, 'We are expecting an increase of 40% in sales but we are prepared to settle for an increase of 30%'. Thus, contingency/tolerance is managed by prioritisation of the features, rather than by adding time or cost tolerances.

Contingency is built into estimates and is not an additional percentage of tolerance.

9.7 Progress reports

An assessment happens at the end of each phase, based on a progress report, where the client assesses the continued viability of the project and, if satisfied, gives the development team approval to proceed with the next phase (or stage).

The client must be aware of the need to avoid technical or irrelevant discussions and to focus on the management aspects which, when taken as a whole, inform the decision on whether to proceed or not. As a rule of thumb, an end phase review should not last more than two hours. The team lead will have been in touch with the client, making sure that they know what is coming and finding out what they think about the future of the project. 'No surprises' is the best way to ensure short progress reports and reviews.

Of course, the 'bottom line' is whether the project is still predicted to deliver sufficient benefits to justify the investment, i.e. is the project justification still sound?

9.8 Information radiators

I described these in section 2.2, I recommend their use. Information radiators should be big, visible, unavoidable and able to convey information at a glance from across the room.

If we enlarge the concept to include identified risks and issues, our PM4A logs for these become more open. The concept is to have this information available on physical noticeboards for all to see, rather than in electronic form where visibility is less easy to achieve. This includes the client and therefore reduces or removes the need for progress reports.

9.9 Action log

Risks are examined:

- Before starting the project;
- Before commencing a new phase;
- As part of the analysis of any major change; and
- Before confirming project closure.

Ideally the action log should be displayed on the information radiator so that its information can be seen by all.

9.10 Problem reports

Requests for change or discovered errors that cannot be dealt with in the current work package are simply returned to the PRL for re-prioritisation. If a situation arises where it becomes clear that there is a danger of not including all the 'Must haves' within the project work package, a problem report must be sent immediately to the client, detailing the problem, options and a recommendation.

9.11 Work packages

A work package is an agreement between the development team members to undertake a piece of work – an iteration or timebox in Agile terms. It describes the work and products required, agreed dates, standards to be used and quality requirements. No work should start without team approval, so it is a powerful schedule, cost and quality control for the project.

9.12 Stand-up meetings

This is a short progress meeting by the development team, held daily, normally lasting 15 minutes or less, describing:

- What they have done since yesterday's stand-up;
- What they intend to do today; and
- Any problems, risks or issues.

Together with the information radiator, they dispense with the need for formal written reports. Because the user (product owner) is part of the team, there is a continuous flow of progress information to the stakeholders.

Common pitfalls of stand-up meetings

- Perhaps the most common mistake is to turn the daily meeting into a 'status report' with each member reporting progress to the same person (the team lead). Exchanges in the daily meeting should be on a peer-to-peer basis.
- A second common pitfall is a daily meeting that drags on and on; this is easy to address with a modicum of facilitation skills.

- A third common issue is a team finding little value in the daily meeting, to the point where people will 'forget' to have it unless the team lead takes the initiative; this often reveals a lukewarm commitment to the reporting structure.

- One final common symptom: the 'no problem' meeting, where no team member ever raises obstacles, even though the team is manifestly not delivering peak performance; this is sometimes an indication that the corporate culture makes people uncomfortable with discussing difficulties in a group setting.

CHAPTER 10: TECHNIQUES

This is what Agile says

Agile has a looser definition of what a technique is. Sometimes it is a meeting, sometimes a management product and sometimes a way of working. Let me explain by looking at two slightly different explanations of Agile techniques.

Lucidchart lists some Agile techniques as:

- **Plan.** The sprint begins with a sprint planning meeting, where team members come together to lay out components for the upcoming round of work. The product manager prioritizes work from a backlog of tasks to assign the team.

- **Develop.** Design and develop the product in accordance with the approved guidelines.

- **Test/QA.** Complete thorough testing and documentation of results before delivery.

- **Deliver.** Present the working product or software to stakeholders and customers.

- **Assess.** Solicit feedback from the customer and stakeholders and gather information to incorporate into the next sprint.[15]

A second approach has a different list specific to the Scrum technique:

---

[15] *www.lucidchart.com/blog/agile-software-development-life-cycle*.

Scrum is a management framework for incremental product development using one or more cross-functional, self-organizing teams of about seven people each.

Scrum provides a structure of roles, meetings, rules, and artifacts. Teams are responsible for creating and adapting their processes within this framework.

Scrum uses fixed-length iterations, called Sprints, which are typically two weeks or 30 days long. Scrum teams attempt to build a potentially shippable (properly tested) product increment every iteration.[16]

Prioritised backlog and product backlog are obviously the same. Both lists contain retrospectives (see section 2.6 for an explanation). Sprint planning and iteration planning are two names for the same thing.

This is what PM4A says

PM4A has a tighter definition of what a technique is. It has only two definitions: product-based planning and quality review.

The difference matters because …

We need to sort out our use of terminology. There is too much confusion in Agile over the use of the word 'technique' and too much jargon. Our method will stick to the two PM4A techniques, cover meetings in the *Progress* chapter and put ways of planning in the *Plans* chapter.

---

[16] *www.agilestrategicsolutions.com/wp-content/uploads/2014/09/Six-Pages-About-Scrum.pdf.*

Here is what APM should do

APM explains six techniques to be used in the life of the project:

1. MoSCoW prioritisation.
2. Modelling.
3. Product-based planning.
4. Iterative development.
5. Timeboxing.
6. Quality reviews.

Product-based planning is covered in the *Plans* chapter and the quality review technique is covered in the *Quality* chapter.

10.1 MoSCoW prioritisation

It is necessary before looking further into planning to understand the MoSCoW principle. MoSCoW stands for:

MoSCow prioritisation

M – MUST have this time

S – SHOULD have this if at all possible

C – COULD have this if it does not affect anything else

W – WON'T have this time but WOULD like this in the future

10.1.1 Must haves

- Fundamental to the end product.
- Without them the end product will be unworkable or useless.

- Minimum usable subset.
- Guaranteed to be delivered.

10.1.2 Should haves

- Important requirements.
- Not absolutely essential. Would add a lot of value to the end product; but there is a workaround in the short term.

10.1.3 Could haves

- Would add business benefit.
- More easily left out than 'Should haves'.

10.1.4 Won't haves

Valuable but can wait until a later enhancement.

Case study example

If we think back to our case study, we can see some possible MoSCoW decisions:

Case study

- The new health and safety regulations are a 'Must have'.
- The certificates are a 'Should have', in that we can proceed as long as we have the test results and supply the certificates at a later date if time runs out.
- The web-based course itself is a 'Must have', having made the decision to use this approach, but within the work to deliver the course, we could have the health and safety information as 'Must haves', but presentation,

---

> font usage, background colours and other 'dressing up'
> as 'Could haves.'

Work is continually re-prioritised on this basis to ensure that the available work is focused on what brings most value to the users. Clearly, the initial aim is to satisfy all requirements, including changes that arrive during the project life cycle, but delivering on a required date without compromising quality may mean that some of what was originally envisaged for delivery may have to be left out. Essential work must be done and only less critical work omitted.

The 'Must haves' on their own must form a coherent solution. If not, then whatever 'lower priority' features are needed to form a coherent solution must be regarded as 'Must haves'.

Work packages should contain a mixture of 'Must haves', 'Should haves' and 'Could haves' to give the flexibility of what can be dropped in order to meet the deadline. It is the de-scoping of lower priority requirements that enables teams to deliver on time when problems arise.

10.2 Modelling

A model can be defined as:

- A description or an analogy used to help visualise something that cannot be directly observed;
- A small but exact copy of something; or
- A pattern or figure of something to be made.

Modelling can be used to:

- Gain a common understanding of requirements;
- Confirm expectations; and
- Test the achievability of objectives.

Prototyping is a kind of modelling, but a model may not be a prototype. A prototype may be an early vision of what the final product might look or act like. A model may be presented in a diagram with its own rules and symbols. You can model an existing situation, whereas a prototype usually implies a new structure.

What is a Prototype?

- An incomplete part of the total solution.
- Used to learn more about what is required.
- Evolutionary (evolving into the final solution) or disposable.
- The intent is to build something visible, valuable and working as soon as possible.

Models or prototypes help communication to ensure that we are on the right track or give the users a vision of what the end product will be like. They are used to make elements of the product visible as early as possible. The danger is in getting carried away and spending too much time on the detail of the model beyond what is needed to satisfy its purpose. A model may deliberately omit some details to provide a clearer focus on another aspect. An example would be the London Underground map, showing the lines and stations, but ignoring the different levels, signals, wiring, etc.

A product flow diagram is an example of a model of a project's work.

10.2.1 Modelling in the project lifecycle

In the *Propose* phase, a model could offer a 'big picture' to convey the scope and essence of the project subject. If we take our sample case study, we might present the model in Figure 10.1 to show the basic products of the project.

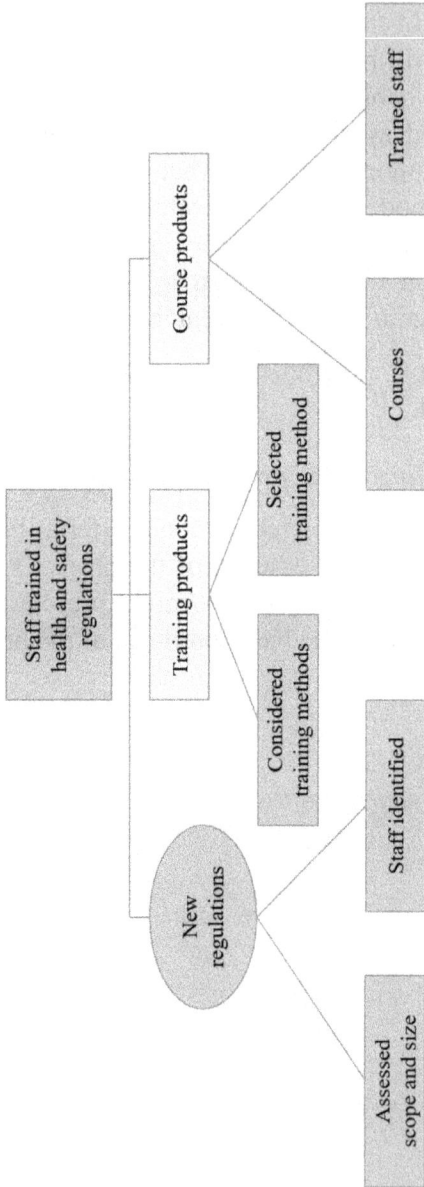

Figure 10.1: Case study model

In the *Plan* phase we might make use of a model to discuss with the users the options for the project approach. The model shows the possibilities of creating a computer-based course, a lecture course or a booklet to explain the new regulations. At the end a certificate would be awarded to those who have undergone the training.

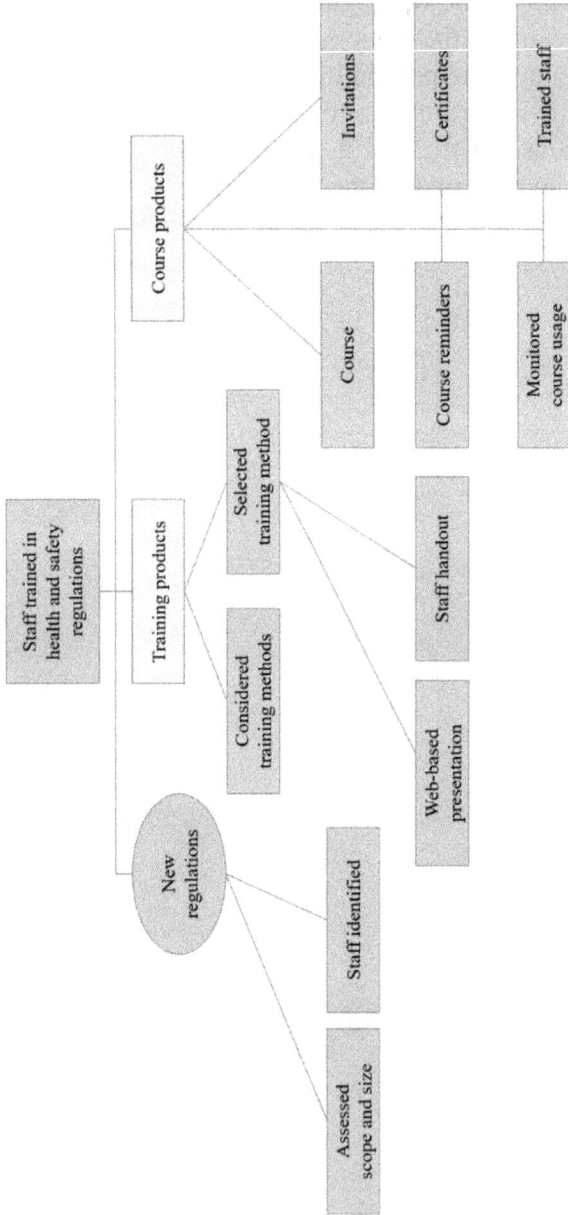

Figure 10.2: Case study model product breakdown structure

10.3 Product-based planning

Product-based planning is a recommended planning technique. There are two reasons for this. Firstly, a project delivers products, not activities, so why begin at a lower level? The second reason is quality. We can measure the quality of a product. The quality of an activity can only be measured by the quality of its outcome (the product).

Product-based planning has three key components:

1. Product breakdown structure.
2. Product descriptions.
3. Product flow diagram.

10.3.1 Product breakdown structure

A product breakdown structure is a hierarchy of the products that the plan is required to produce. At the top of the hierarchy is the final end product, e.g. a computer system, a new yacht, a department relocated to a new building. This is then broken down into its major constituents at the next level. Each constituent is then broken down into its parts, and this process continues until the planner has reached the level of detail required for the plan.

There can be three types of 'product' in a product breakdown structure.

10.3.1.1 Simple products

Products at the lowest level of any branch of the hierarchy are 'simple products'. The number of levels in a product breakdown structure depends on the level of detail required to allow the client, project or team manager to exercise an appropriate level of control. Simple products are shown in the diagrams inside a rectangle.

10.3.1.2 Intermediate products

'Intermediate product' is a term used to describe everything that appears in a product breakdown structure between the final product and the simple products at the bottom of the various branches of the hierarchy.

An intermediate product may be a 'real' product, such as one where activities such as assembly or testing must be applied to that product after the simple products below it have been produced. Such products will appear in the product flow diagram and a product description must be written for them.

Other intermediate products may not be 'real' products, but memory joggers for a group of simple products. An example of such a 'product' might be 'required tools'; not a product in itself but used as a starting point to think of real products, such as drill, drill bits, hammer. This type of intermediate product is **not** carried forward into the product flow diagram, nor is a product description written for it.

Intermediate products are also drawn in the diagrams in a rectangle.

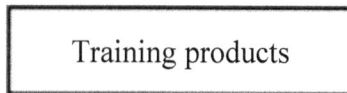

```
┌─────────────────────────────────────┐
│        Training products             │
└─────────────────────────────────────┘
```

10.3.1.3 External products

Apart from the products that a project must create or obtain, it may rely on products that already exist or products that are to be provided by another project. A key question to recognising that a product is external is to ask if the project has control over its creation. As an example, a company may have a standard template that is used for all invitations to tender. If yours is a procurement project, you will gather a list of your specific requirements and then use the company template as the basis for your invitation to suppliers. The template would be an external product to your project because it already exists. Take another example; your project is building an office and you will need connection to a telephone line. This will be supplied by a specialist telephone company and you have no control over the telephone staff nor do you develop the telephone connection product.

A different symbol should be used to identify external products. An ellipse (see Figure 10.3) is used in the example in this book to indicate an external product in both the product breakdown structure and the product flow diagram. It should be noted that it is the product that is shown, not the source of the product. For example, if a plan needs an electric generator, 'electric generator' would be the external product, not the relevant manufacturer of the generator.

Having described external products, just a word of warning. You may have external suppliers building and providing some of your project products to specifications that you provide. They are under the control of the project as a development team, so the products involved are not external, they are developed as part of your project. Just because a supplier is external does not mean that the products they create for your project are external products.

Case study

In our case study, the health and safety 'new regulations' would be an external product, one over which the project has no control.

10.3.2 Product description

For each significant product, at all levels of the product breakdown structure, a description is produced. Its creation forces the planner to consider if enough is known about the product in order to plan its production. It is also the first time that the quality of the product is considered. The quality criteria indicate how much and what type of quality checking will be required.

The purposes of this are, therefore, to provide a guide:

- To the planner in how much effort will be required to create the product;
- To the author of the product on what is required; and
- Against which the finished product can be measured.

These descriptions are a vital checklist to be used at a quality check of the related products.

The description should contain:

- The purpose of the product;
- The products from which it is derived;
- The composition of the product;
- Any standards for format and presentation;
- The quality criteria to be applied to the product; and
- The quality verification method to be used.

The product description is given to both the product's creator and those who will verify its quality.

Case study example product description

Product description			
Product	**Staff identified**	**Version no.**	**0.1**

Purpose
To identify staff who require training in the new health and safety regulations.

Composition
Heading, staff name, ID, job, grade, location, area affected.

Derivation
HR department staff list. *Health and safety new regulations.* *Assessed scope.*

Format and presentation
List including composition fields plus extra fields for contacted and trained. Arial font size 12.

Quality tolerance
All quality criteria must be met 100%.

Heading should indicate list project and purpose.		
Quality criteria	Checked by P. Owner	Checked by HR rep
No staff missing who are affected by the new rules.		
Names correctly spelt.		
Correct IDs and location.		

Quality method

Inspection by checkers against complete staff list.

Quality responsibilities

Role	Responsible individuals
Product creator	*Development team*
Product reviewer(s)	*HR rep*
Product approver(s)	*Senior users*

10.3.3 Product flow diagram

A product flow diagram is a diagram showing the sequence in which products must be produced and the dependencies between them.

A product flow diagram normally needs only three symbols: a rectangle to contain products developed within the plan, an ellipse for external products and an arrow to show the dependencies.

10.3.4 Case study project plan example

Case study

Our case study is a project whose objective is to devise a course to train the company's staff in some new health and safety regulations (see chapter 3).

A presentation to the staff needs to be created and a handbook on the new regulations will be given to each staff member who completes the course. You will have to find out from the HR department which members of staff need to go on the course. Each attendee will receive a certificate of attendance and a list of trained staff will be passed back to the HR department. In making the plan, you are aware that legislation is still being finalised and this may cause late additions to material and the number of staff to be trained.

The development team has no control over the creation of the new regulations, so this is an external product.

Later in the *Propose* phase, more detail will be available for consideration of the project approach.

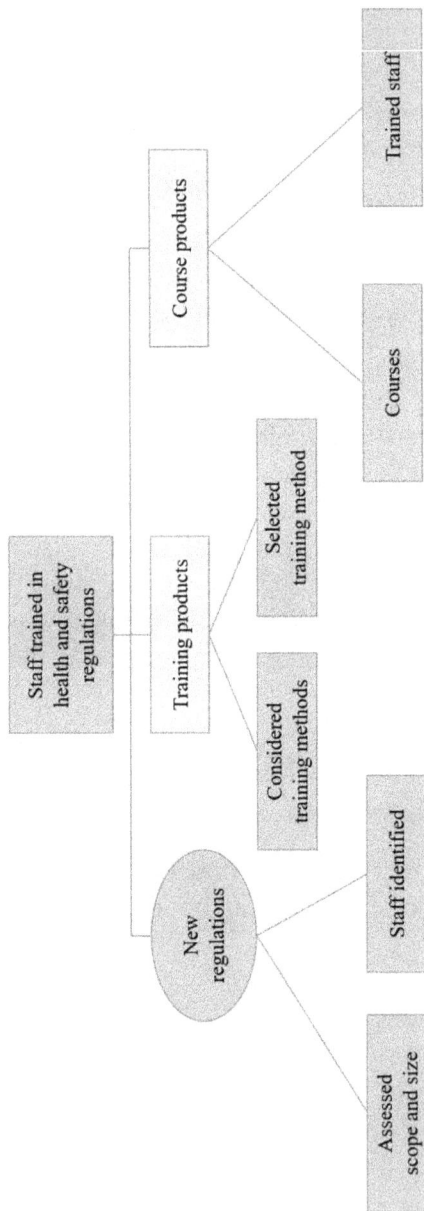

Figure 10.3: More detail appears

You will note that 'training products' and 'course products' are not actual products, just memory joggers, and are not carried forward into any product flow diagram.

At the end of initiation, the start-up team should be able to present a project plan such as the ones in Figures 10.4 and 10.5.

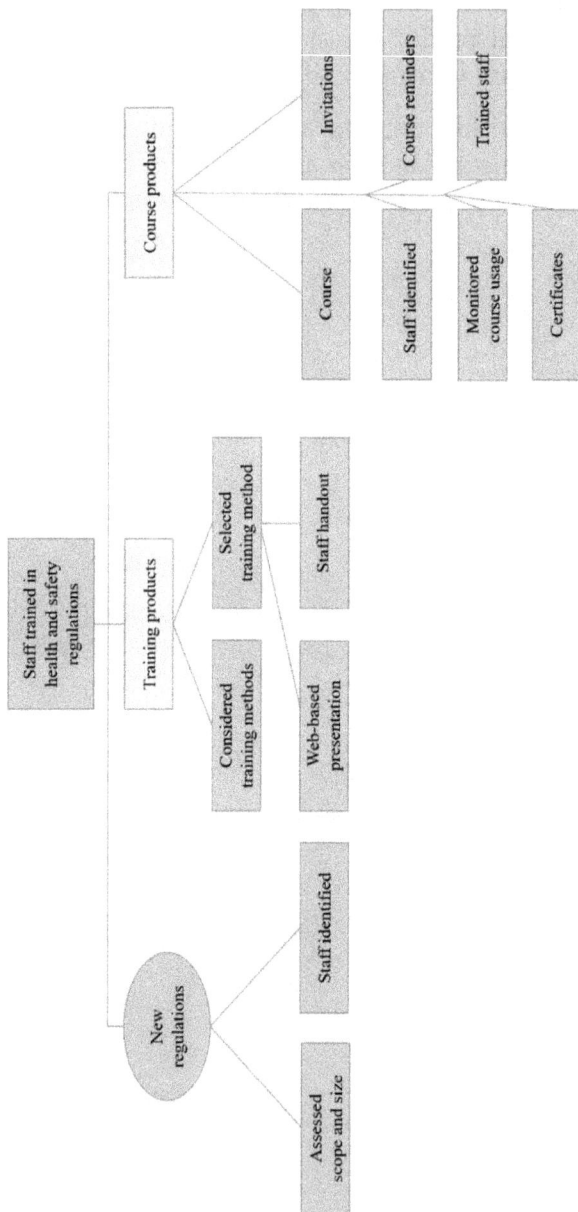

Figure 10.4: Final project plan

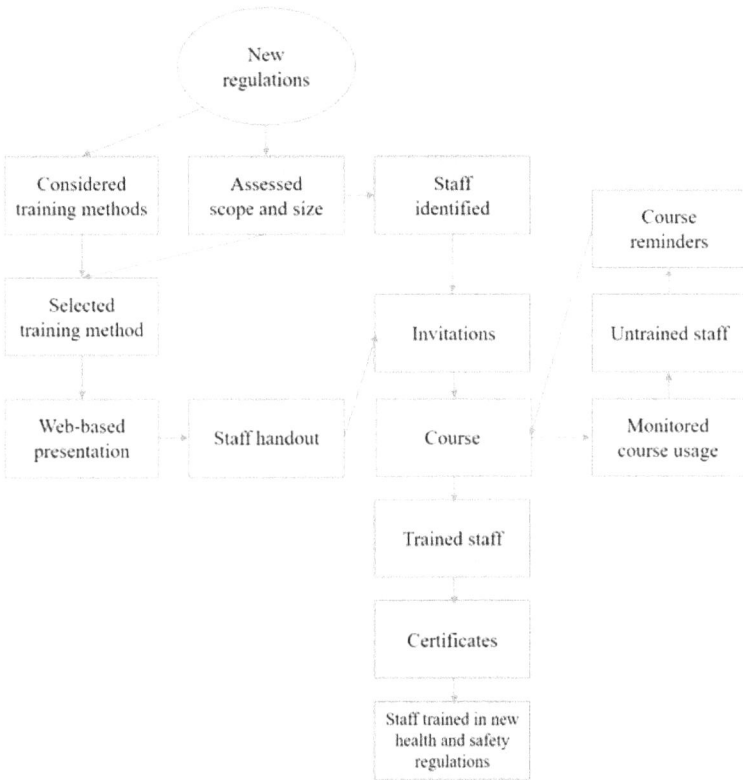

Figure 10.5: Project product flow diagram

An assumption is made here that identification of the staff that need training will be part of the project, not provided by an external source.

10.4 Iterative development

Iterative development is a fundamental part of APM. It allows the high-level requirements established during the *Propose* and *Plan* phases to be explored and evolve in increasing detail during the planning stages and work packages. It includes a feedback loop into the next iteration.

Iterative development cycles are short, typically days or even hours. The steps within iteration are:

- **Identify** – the team agrees the objective of the work.
- **Plan** – the team works out what needs to be done, by whom, to meet that objective.
- **Evolve** – the team work on the solution.
- **Review** – the work is tested to see if the objective has been met.

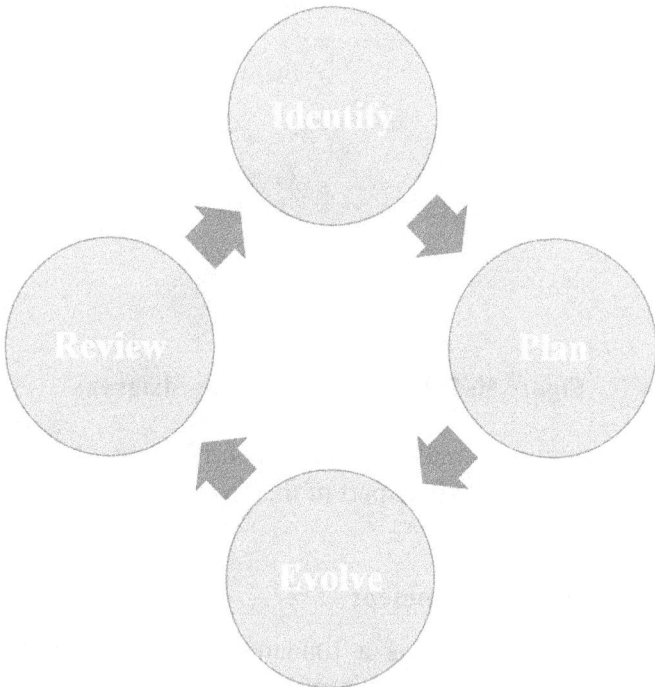

Figure 10.6: The iteration cycle

Anything planned for delivery but not completed within the work package must be addressed. It may be agreed by the development team to become a 'Won't have'; or it may be included in a later work package, but something else may need to be de-scoped to include this. If 'Must have' requirements have not been completed, re-planning should include these in exchange for later 'Could haves' or 'Should haves'. This is done during the re-prioritisation in the *Create* phase at the end of each stage.

Management of the iterative development cycle is achieved through:

- Timeboxed work packages;
- Change control (together with MoSCoW prioritisation);
- Version control; and
- Quality testing.

Iterative development is dependent on continuous involvement and feedback from the product owner role.

10.5 Timebox

This is a finite period for work to be carried out to meet an objective or deliver a product. It is a key concept that the time allowed is never extended. Instead, the work allocated is prioritised and done in that order (see MoSCoW in section 10.1). If all the work is not complete by the end of the timebox, the unfinished part is returned to the PRL to be re-prioritised, and re-estimated or sized to reflect the remaining effort required.

Key points:

- The work in the timebox is to deliver the selected features.

- Timeboxes should also be used for work other than work packages, such as identifying the project approach and defining the business case.

10.6 Quality review

A quality review is a team method of checking the quality of something by a review process. It applies to all documents and products created by the project in order for the end products to be accepted by the users. For simplicity's sake, we will refer to these as 'products', given that, for example, the project mandate and project justification, etc. are also 'products' that need quality checking. Knowing that a product has been checked and declared error-free, provides a more confident basis to move ahead and use that product as the basis of future work. It is also a requirement of ISO – the International Organisation for Standardization – that the client at any time can check a project's quality records.

The purpose of a quality review is to gain sign-off or approval that a product is 'fit for purpose'. The objective is to inspect a product for errors in a planned, independent, controlled and documented manner, and ensure that any errors found are fixed. It needs to be used with common sense to avoid the dangers of an over-bureaucratic approach, but with the intent to follow the process laid down (to ensure nothing is missed).

Quality review documentation should be filed with the product description to provide a record that the product was inspected, that any errors found were corrected and that the corrections were themselves checked, reviewed and signed off. All products must pass a quality review and be signed off for the end products to be accepted by the client.

10.6.1 Quality review planning

Quality reviews, which occur in the *Create* phase, are planned during the *Plan* phase. The planning includes not only the moment when a quality review should be applied to a product, but also the resources to be used and their roles as part of the review.

10.6.2 People involvedin a quality review

The parties whose interests should be **considered** when drawing up a list of attendees required at a quality review are:

- The creator(s) of the product;
- The client;
- Those who will use, operate or maintain the end product;
- Members of staff whose work will be affected by the end product;
- Specialists in the relevant end product area; and
- Any business or developer standards representatives.

The first two of these, the creator and the client, are members of the project team. The remainder are likely to be people from outside the project team, users and/or stakeholders.

10.6.3 Quality review roles and steps

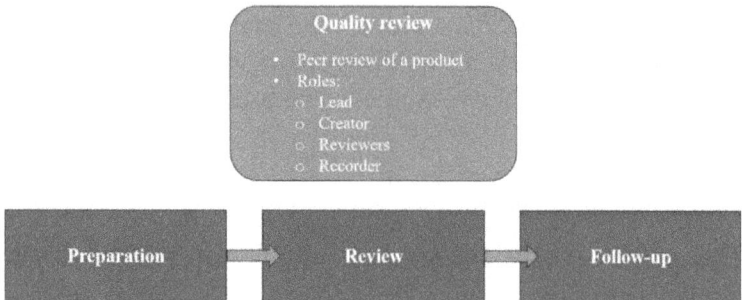

Figure 10.7: Quality review roles and steps

The roles involved in a typical quality review are:

- **The lead** – the person responsible for ensuring that the quality review is properly organised and controlled.
- **The creator(s)** of the product being reviewed –*t*his role must ensure that the reviewers have all the required information to perform their role at the review. This means forwarding a copy of the product description to them during the preparation step, and, if physically possible, a copy of the product to be reviewed and any other documents needed to put it in context. The creator must then answer any questions about the product or document during the review so a decision can be reached on whether the product is 'fit for purpose' or not. If not, then the creator will do most, if not all, of the correcting work – 'follow-on-actions'. The creator must not be allowed to be defensive about the product.
- **Reviewer(s)** – one or more people who have either a

vested interest in the quality of the product or who have the skills and experience necessary to assess the quality of the product.

- **A recorder** – Someone to take notes of what happened at the review, and any follow-on-actions required, etc.

It must be remembered that these are roles ...

Must all be represented at a quality review, but again, depending on the size of your business and type of project, a person may take on more than one role.

10.6.4 Quality review steps

There are three distinct steps within the quality review procedure: preparation, review and follow-up.

Step 1 – Preparation

The objective of this step is for the reviewers to examine the product under review and to create a question list for the review.

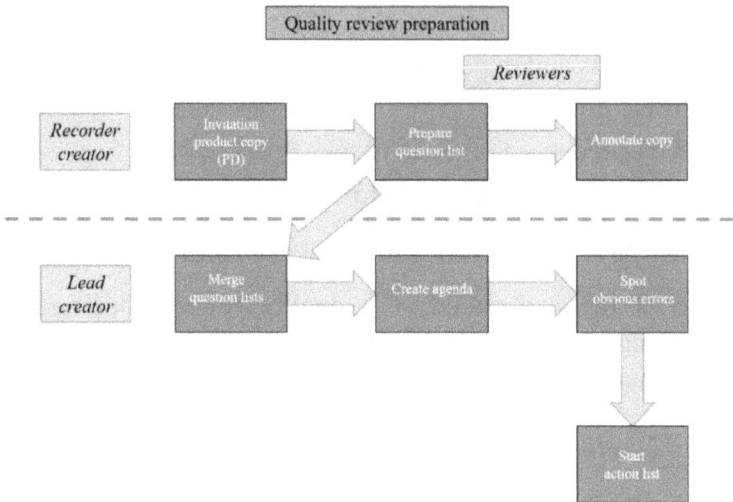

Figure 10.8: Quality review preparation

The lead checks that the product is ready for its planned review. The recorder sends out an invitation to the reviewers. The creator must provide a copy of the product description and the product (or its location where copying the product is impractical) to each reviewer.

Each reviewer will compare the product and any supporting documents against the product description; annotate the product with any typos, grammar or other minor errors; and fill in a question list of any points where they feel there is a mistake or they have a question.

The question lists are submitted to the creator, who discusses them with the lead before the review. The questions are collated to form an agenda. The creator may be able to see that some of the questions identify errors in the product and will need corrective work. These can be put on an action list and placed at the top of the agenda to be acknowledged as errors at the review, thus avoiding needless discussion.

Step 2 – Review

The objective of the review is to either agree that a product is 'fit for purpose' and can be 'signed off', or to agree an action list of any follow-on work required, if any, that may be needed to correct the product. The lead and the creator do not have to resolve these actions at the meeting – it is sufficient for the lead and reviewers to agree that a particular item needs correction or at least re-work. Provided that the action is logged, the reviewers have an opportunity in the next step to confirm that corrective action has been taken and that the action has resolved the problem. The product description is updated with the actual date and result of the review. The product copies are returned to the creator, who will correct any minor typos. These should not need discussion. At the end of the review the lead should add to each item on the action list the name(s) of the reviewers who wish to confirm that the correction has been done.

Step 3 – Follow-up

The objective of the follow-up step is to ensure that all actions identified on the action list during the review step have been dealt with.

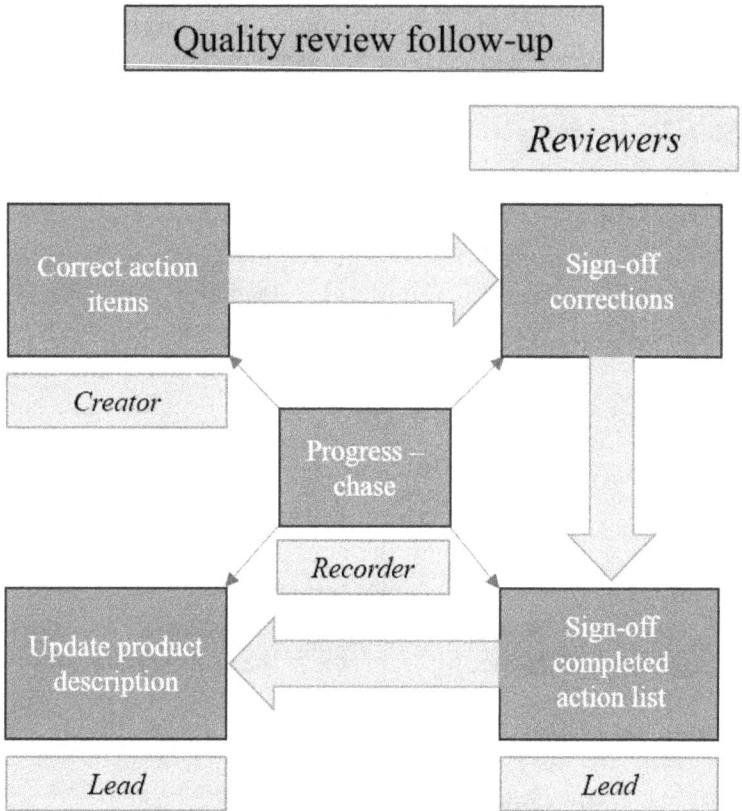

Figure 10.9: Quality review follow-up

The person who has the role of recorder will 'progress chase' the other people involved to ensure that there are no delays in the corrective work and that everything is done.

When an error has been fixed, the creator will obtain sign-off from whoever is nominated on the action list. This person may be the reviewer who raised the initial query, but other reviewers also have the option of checking the correction.

When all errors have been reconciled and sign-off obtained, the lead will confirm that the product is complete, sign off the action list and notify the project manager of the result. At this point the version number of the product is updated to reflect its sign-off and approval, and the product version control records are updated with the date of final sign-off (see section 14.4). The schedule is updated accordingly to reflect the outcome of the review.

10.6.5 Formal and informal reviews

A variation on a formal review is to have the reviewers submit their question lists but the actual review is only done by the lead and the creator.

Depending on the size of the project and business, quality reviews can be either formal (that is, a scheduled meeting conducted as described above) or informal (that is, a 'get-together' between two people to informally review a product).

Informal quality reviews follow a similar format to the formal quality review and the paperwork emerging from both meetings is similar. The main difference is the number of people involved, the informality of the proceedings during the three steps and the overall time required. As a minimum, a quality review requires two people: one to take the roles of the lead and the reviewer, the other to take the roles of the creator and recorder.

CHAPTER 11: INTRODUCTION TO THE PROCESSES

Agile says:

There are several descriptions of Agile phases. Figure 11.1 represents a general view of them.

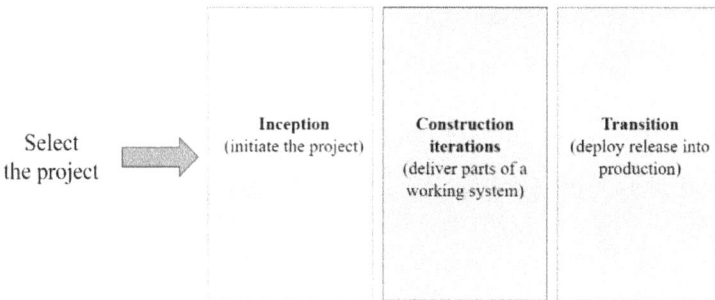

| Select the project | Inception (initiate the project) | Construction iterations (deliver parts of a working system) | Transition (deploy release into production) |

Figure 11.1: Typical Agile phases

Agile diagrams often show a pre-project iteration Inception) where the project is selected. I believe that this work is not part of the project but is part of a higher-level task, and part of a company's strategic thinking and planning. ISO 21500:2012, Guidance on project management, shows creation of a project business case as part of the work in portfolio management, and deciding which potential project to select.

PM4A says:

PM4A has four phases. The *Propose* and *Plan* phases combined are the equivalent of the Agile inception phase. The *Close* phase is the equivalent of the Agile transition phase. A project may have many stages in the *Create* phase during which products are developed, but the diagram in Figure 11.2 does not clearly show these iterations in the *Create* phase.

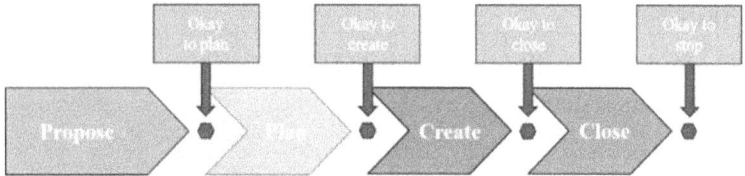

Figure 11.2: PM4A phases

The difference matters because ...

The PM4A process diagram does not show the conveyor belt philosophy of regularly delivering working products and benefits throughout the project life cycle.

Here is what APM should do:

Building the right product to meet business need is of primary importance. The key is to maximise business benefit by delivering essential functionality within tight timescales through controlling how much is developed, rather than extending the time allotted or allowing the quality to be compromised. These objectives are achieved by:

- Iterative development and prototyping;
- Focusing on high-priority features that will deliver maximum business benefit;
- Active business involvement;
- Empowerment of the team; and
- Frequent product and/or benefit delivery.

The phases are shown in Figure 11.3 below:

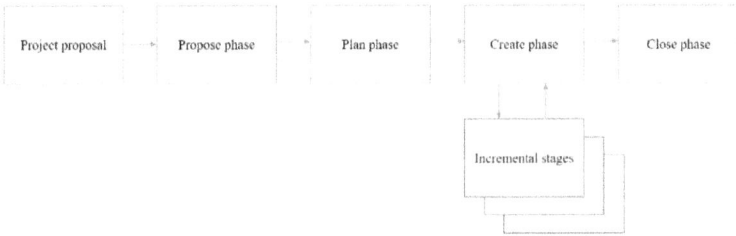

Figure 11.3: All the phases

CHAPTER 12: THE PROPOSE PHASE

A project is triggered by the issue of a project proposal. This should state 'this is the objective; this is the money we have; this is the time we have'. The task of the *Propose* phase is to assess the practicality of the project in terms of cost and to develop alternative options.

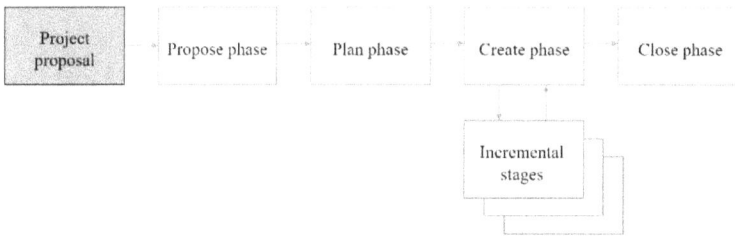

Figure 12.1: Locating the *Propose* phase

It is recognised that this is based on limited information about the project plus knowledge of similar solutions and projects.

12.1 Purpose

In summary, the purposes of the *Propose* phase are to:

- Get an idea of what the project is to do (from the project proposal);
- Nominate the client;
- Appoint the start-up and initiation team;
- Create a daily log and action log;
- Identify the users of the end product;

- Identify other interested parties (stakeholders);
- Identify the business reasons for the project;
- Check the scope is clear;
- Examine alternative solutions and select;
- Complete the project mandate;
- Identify communication requirements; and
- Plan the next phase.

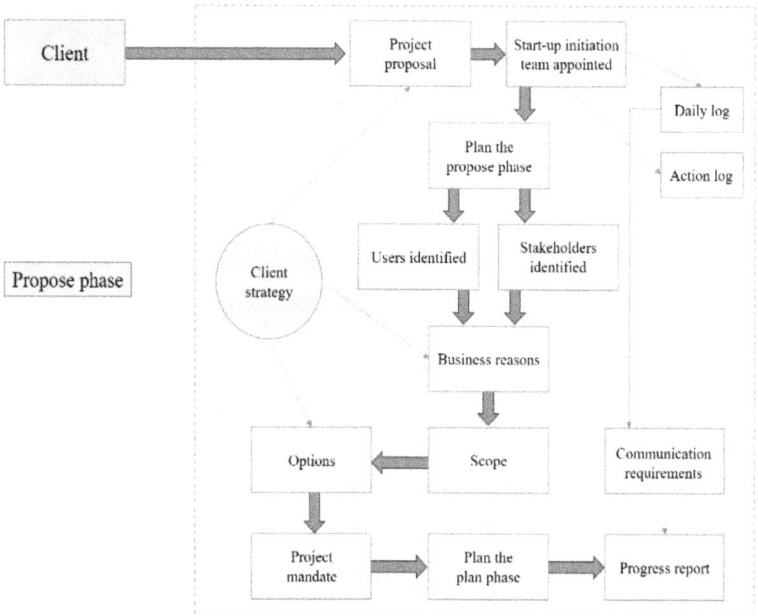

Figure 12.2: Starting up a project

12.1.1 APM principles supported

The principle of business need is supported in this phase.

12.2 Project proposal

'Project proposal' is the term used in PM4A to describe the trigger for a project. It is triggered when a business change is proposed, such as an idea for a new product or a change to an existing product or service – an end product that could benefit the business. It may be in the format of a full specification of a problem, a brief written request to 'look into' something or 'do something about ...', or even a verbal request.

If we are very lucky, a full project proposal will have been provided, which will include:

- The background to the project;
- Project objectives;
- Project scope; and
- Business reasons for the project –The business must believe there are good reasons for undertaking the project if it is to commit to the first phase of the project – the *Propose* phase.

12.3 Nominate the client

If the business believes the proposal is worth looking into, someone needs to be appointed to represent the business interests – the client. The role of the client also has a duty to gather and prioritise the users' requirements of the end product and ensure that these requirements are met by the project. Depending on the size of the business, the client may be the owner of the business, for example, the managing director; a business partner; a member of the board of directors; or a manager with sufficient budgetary authority. Because of the level of authority and budgetary responsibility given to the client, this person must be appropriate for the role. They will usually hold a responsible position in the business, and/or have a vested interest in the project's success.

The person appointed to role of the client will:

- Hold the purse strings for the project;
- Be ultimately responsible for the project's success;
- Have the decision-making authority for the project;
- Ensure the project meets business strategies;
- Ensure the end product meets user requirements; and
- Ensure it is worth spending the time and effort to complete the *Propose* phase and *proceed* to the next phase.

12.4 Appoint the start-up and initiation team

The client's first task is to appoint the start-up and initiation team. This team will complete the work of this phase. (In small and medium-sized projects this team may be the same as the development team.)

The content of the project proposal should give an indication of the background skills and knowledge that the team will need.

The team will then carry out the following activities.

12.5 Plan the *Propose* phase work

The first job of the team is to create a plan for the *Propose* phase work. This will be the start of the project plan, but at this point will just cover the *Propose* phase work.

12.6 Identify who will be the users of the end product

The team should identify with the client the users for whom the end product is intended. The users of the end product need to be identified, because they will provide useful input to the reasons and justification for the product and specify their requirements for the end product.

12.7 Identify the stakeholders

Stakeholders are those who have an interest in the end product, or will be affected by it, or the work of the project. They have an interest, but they are not decisionmakers as far as the project is concerned. The client should help identify any stakeholders.

The type and shape of alternative solutions will have an impact on people other than the users. The input of all interested parties needs to be gathered so they can be consulted about the alternative solutions selection of the chosen solution.

12.8 Create an action log

The action log (see appendix A.1) will contain a summary of all project risks and issues raised during the project to enable them to be tracked. A full detailed description of risks and issues will be recorded in the risk reports and project issue forms (see appendix A.9 and A.13). The action log should be created by the team on day one, ready to capture any noteworthy events, risks or issues.

The project proposal and project mandate should be scrutinised for any identified risks to the project.

12.9 Check there are valid reasons for the project

The main intention of checking the project proposal is to avoid wasting resources on projects for which no valid business reasons exist.

The team carries out a more detailed investigation to understand the background, objectives and the business reasons for the project as, hopefully, defined in the project proposal. Otherwise, this information is obtained from an interview with the client, a feasibility study or any other documents.

At this early time, only the reasons for wanting the project may be known. You may be lucky and find there was an earlier feasibility study that estimated some of the expected benefits, but beware, these are notoriously optimistic.

It is always worthwhile finding out the reasons for the project and doing a little common-sense check on the validity of these. A check of the business strategy is one place to start. It stops you from being embarrassed when management ask, "Why are you doing this project?"

If we take our example project, health and safety training, the reason for our project is that the government is introducing new legislation in which hospital staff need to be trained.

12.10 Check that the scope of the project is clear

'Scope' is a statement that defines the boundaries of the project. Scope indicates not only what will be done, but also what will not be done.

Here is a quote from the *Sunday Telegraph Business Reporter* in March 2017:

> Although it sounds simple to ensure projects have a clear direction and goal throughout, many struggle as the goalposts are shifted. And while we live in a world where business requirements will change, it is important to ensure the project is properly scoped with a prioritised list of requirements rather than an endless wish-list. The focus should always be on why the project is required, what is the problem that is trying to be solved and a clear vision of what is required to solve it![17]

An example from my days with an oil company is "The scope of the new payroll system includes all paid employees, full or part-time, with the exception of the company directors, whose salary will be dealt with by another system".

The development team checks the needs and scope of the project against business strategies and plans the work needed to obtain any extra information needed.

A review is made of the information provided in the project proposal and the information required in order to complete the phase. Any gaps must be filled.

12.11 Identify and evaluate alternative options

At this point there may be a number of options available to meet the project's objectives.

The team is responsible for reviewing these options and will consult with the client and stakeholders to agree on the

---

[17] *www.business-reporter.co.uk/2017/03/05/expert-panel-key-delivering-projects-time-budget/#gsc.tab=0.*

chosen option. The options fall into two categories: do nothing or do something.

If we take our example project, the main business reason is to train staff in the new health and safety regulations. Alternative options might be:

- Do nothing and carry on as we are; or
- Give each member of staff a copy of the new regulations.

The 'do nothing' option should always be the first business option to consider, because it provides a basis for quantifying the other options, such as, 'What would happen to the business need if nothing was done?', 'What would be the potential losses?', 'What are the costs of continuing as we are today?' These can be compared against the costs and potential savings and benefits of each other option. After the justification for each option has been considered, the chosen option should also be documented in the project mandate (see section 12.12), together with the reasons for choosing it.

The start-up team needs to investigate each option in detail to reach a decision. There are several variables that can be used to examine each alternative option. Here are some suggestions:

- Risks of each option.
- Team size and skills required (and their availability).
- Estimated project duration.
- Estimated cost.
- Assessment of how well the alternative meets the business needs.
- Comparison with business strategy.

In our example project the option chosen was to create on online course.

12.12 Complete the terms of reference for the project (project mandate)

If the project proposal appears to have sufficient merit, the start-up team creates a project mandate (see appendix A.11). The business strategy should be consulted to ensure that the project proposal, project mandate and the chosen solution are in line with it.

The project mandate is a complete set of terms of reference stating:

- The background to the project;
- Objectives of the project;
- Project scope;
- Business reasons for doing the project;
- Any constraints and assumptions;
- Alternative options considered;
- Selected option and reason why it was chosen;
- Reasons why the other options were rejected;
- Details of the users and stakeholders; and
- Estimated project cost and schedule.

It is the basis of the development work to ensure that sufficient information is available for the client to decide on whether to proceed into the *Plan* phase. The project mandate may be a very short, simple document, but it is important as it forms the basis for calculating the project justification. (If the project proposal does not appear to have sufficient merit, the start-up team would advise the client of this, not create a project mandate and recommend that the project should not continue.)

12.13 Identify communication requirements

The development team is responsible for this activity as part of the progress control principle (see chapter 9). It is important to keep all stakeholders informed of project status. Therefore, we need to identify who the interested parties are so that their input can be gathered, and the communication links established.

The start-up team agrees the frequency, content and format (verbal, email, phone, document, etc.) of progress reports with the client (see appendix A.9). The aim in APM is to replace as many reports as possible with the information radiator.

12.14 Plan the *Plan* phase

In order to get approval to move into the *Plan* phase, the start-up team must provide the client with an updated project plan with the actual results and resources used in the *Propose* phase and the products, activities and resources required to carry out the *Plan* phase. The plan should also include a rough estimate of the time and cost for the whole project, taken from the selected option.

12.15 Progress report

As part of the final activity of the *Propose* phase, the start-up team provides a progress report to the client on the performance of the phase. The progress report, together with the completed project mandate and the updated project plan, are given to the client for acceptance and approval to proceed to the next phase.

CHAPTER 13: THE PLAN PHASE

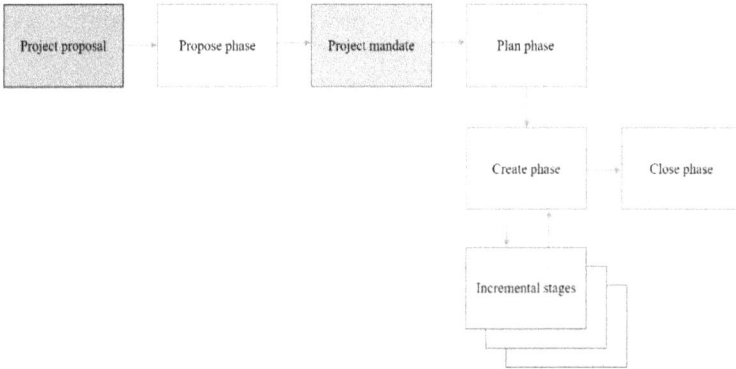

Figure 13.1: Locating the *Plan* phase

13.1 Purpose

The client should reach agreement before major expenditure starts on what is to be done and why it is being done, what quality is required, how long it will take and how much it will cost.

In summary, the purposes of the *Plan* phase are to:

- Identify the quality responsibilities and requirements of the end product (client's quality expectations and acceptance criteria);
- Decide how to implement the selected option (project approach);
- Plan the *Create* phase;
- Agree the tolerance limits (see section 9.6);
- Divide the work into work packages;

- Appoint the project team;
- Verify that the project can be justified (project justification);
- Discuss how the end products will be delivered (handover arrangements);
- Identify how and when the benefits of the project can be measured (post project review plan); and
- Report on progress.

Before we can plan how to create the end product, we need to identify the client's quality expectations. This must be established before we can think about planning the work necessary to achieve that quality and build this into the plan for the next phase – the *Create* phase.

These pieces of information will lead us to design an appropriate project team structure that will be needed to implement the plan and carry out the work.

Having created our plan, we need to create the project justification document that will have all the necessary information needed to prove to the client that it is worthwhile investing the resources for the *Create* phase.

This phase will produce a more detailed estimate for the whole project, now scoped with a PRL. The phase delivers a timed delivery plan based on the MoSCoW technique. The plan must reflect the level of risk and confidence. The 'Should haves' and 'Could haves' represent contingency/tolerances, i.e. if time is running out, one or more of these can be dropped. The focus is on meeting objectives within the allowed time rather than amending time deadlines, and on completing at least the 'Must haves', although time has been allowed for the 'Should haves' and 'Could haves'.

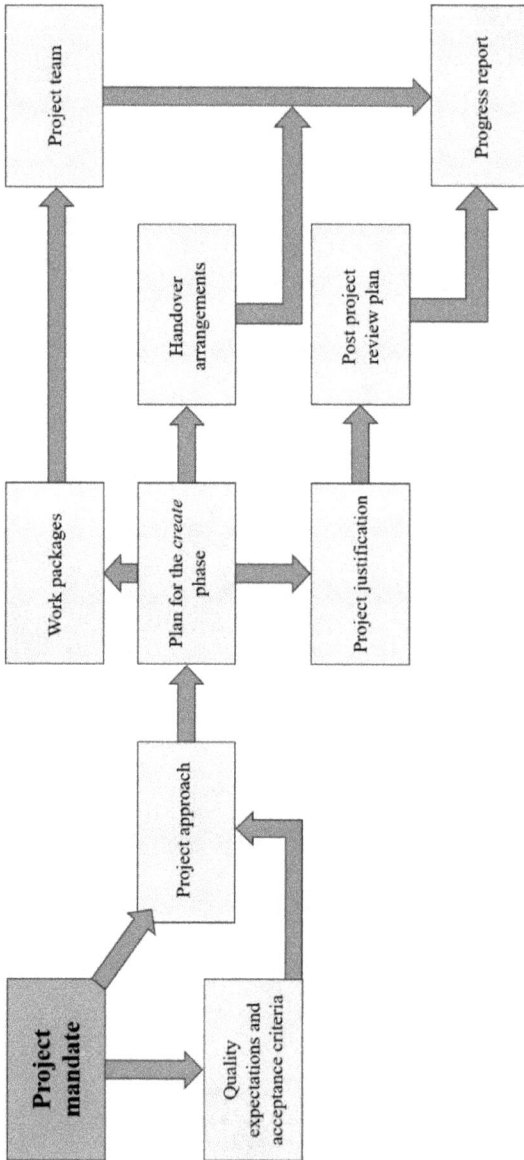

Figure 13.2: The *Plan* phase

13.2 APM principles supported

The principle of *Business Need* is supported by the refinement of the project justification.

Roles are confirmed and some gaps maybe filled in the project development team, supporting the *Collaborate* and *Communicate* principles.

The *Build Incrementally* and *Develop Iteratively* principles are supported by the creation of product descriptions for the major products and the use of the product-based planning technique to create the overall project plan.

13.3 Establish the quality expectations and acceptance criteria

To be successful, the project must deliver a product of the quality expected by the client, as well as meeting time and cost constraints. The required quality and means of achieving that quality must be specified before work begins.

Quality work cannot be planned until the quality expectations of the client are known.

The time and cost of the project will be affected by the amount of quality work that has to be done, therefore, quality work estimates must be done before a realistic release plan can be produced.

The activities needed are:

- The client and start-up team discuss and agree the required quality of the end product;
- Establish what quality standards, tools and techniques will be used; and
- Get the client to define the criteria to be applied for

acceptance of the successful closure of the project.

13.4 Select the project approach

The start-up team is responsible for choosing the project approach. This decides how the selected option in the project mandate will be created.

The alternative project approaches are:

- Build a solution from scratch;
- Take an existing product and modify it;
- Give the job to another business to do for you; and
- Buy a ready-made solution off the shelf.

Choosing the project approach may be very straightforward and obvious, but if not, the following actions may be useful:

- Identify any time, money and resource constraints against possible project approaches.
- Check for any direction or guidance on the project approach from other documents, such as the project proposal, or business strategies and stakeholders.
- Check current industry thinking, and any new technology or tools available for help with ideas for the project approach.
- Identify any security constraints.
- Consider how the product might be brought into use and whether there are any problems that would impact the choice of product approach.
- Produce a range of alternative product approaches.
- Assess the risks in the various product approaches.
- Identify the training needs of the alternative product

approaches and the support that they would require.

The client needs to think very carefully about the project approach proposed by the initiation team. Preparation of the above information can avoid the client being pushed into an approach that is favoured by the project team, but later turns out to have problems for the business, such as lack of flexibility or maintenance difficulties.

The project approach will have an impact on the timescale and costs of the project, plus possibly its scope and quality. Therefore, this information should be made available in the project justification (created later in this phase) for the client to decide whether to continue with the project or not. A note of any discussions and decisions made on the project approach should be recorded in the daily log.

13.5 Plan for the *Create* phase

As part of its decision on whether to proceed with the project, the client needs to know approximately how much the project will cost and how long it will take. Costs from the outline project plan also feed into the business case to help indicate the viability of the project. If the early project work will be to explore if a solution can be found, or what type of solution should be provided, then the outline project plan may only cover the investigation work. If at the end of the investigation a way forward can be proposed, then this would trigger a major revision and extension of the outline project plan.

The actions required are:

- Check if there are any corporate or programme risk strategies, practices and standards that the project should use.

- Review the lessons log for any lessons that relate to risk.

Create a risk management approach for the project, including:

- Procedures to cover identifying, evaluating, assessing, countering, monitoring and communicating risks;
- Risk tools and techniques to be used;
- Records to be kept;
- Risk tolerances; and
- Responsibilities for risk activities.

13.6 Refine the project justification

Before committing to the project it is important to ensure that there is sufficient justification for the resource expenditure and that there is a sound balance between business justification and the risks. Following the point made above, there may have to be a first justification for any investigation work, followed by a new justification based on the proposed solution:

- Check if circumstances and assumptions have changed since the outline business case was created.
- Look for any lessons on the subject of project justification in previous projects.
- Investigate the expected benefits of the project with the client.
- Check with the client for any change to the business reasons for the project.

Create the following project justification:

- Summarise the business options considered and the reasons for selecting the chosen option.
- Quantify the benefits wherever possible.
- Define with the user any tolerances for each benefit.
- Incorporate the costs from the outline project plan.
- Add a summary of the project's major risks.

13.7 Set up a post project review plan

Define measurable criteria for each claimed benefit:

- How the achievement of each benefit is to be measured.
- Capture the measurements of the current situation of each benefit.
- Identify the timing of benefit reviews and the resources that will be required.

13.8 Progress report

As part of the final activity of the *Plan* phase, the start-up team provides a progress report to the client on the performance of the phase. The progress report, together with the completed project justification, the post project review plan and the updated project plan, are given to the client for acceptance and approval to proceed to the next phase.

CHAPTER 14: THE CREATE PHASE

14.1 Summary

The purpose of the *Create* phase is to create and develop products and confirm they meet the client's quality expectations and acceptance criteria. The production of the products within budget, schedule and to the required quality, must be driven by the project manager and requires careful monitoring and control.

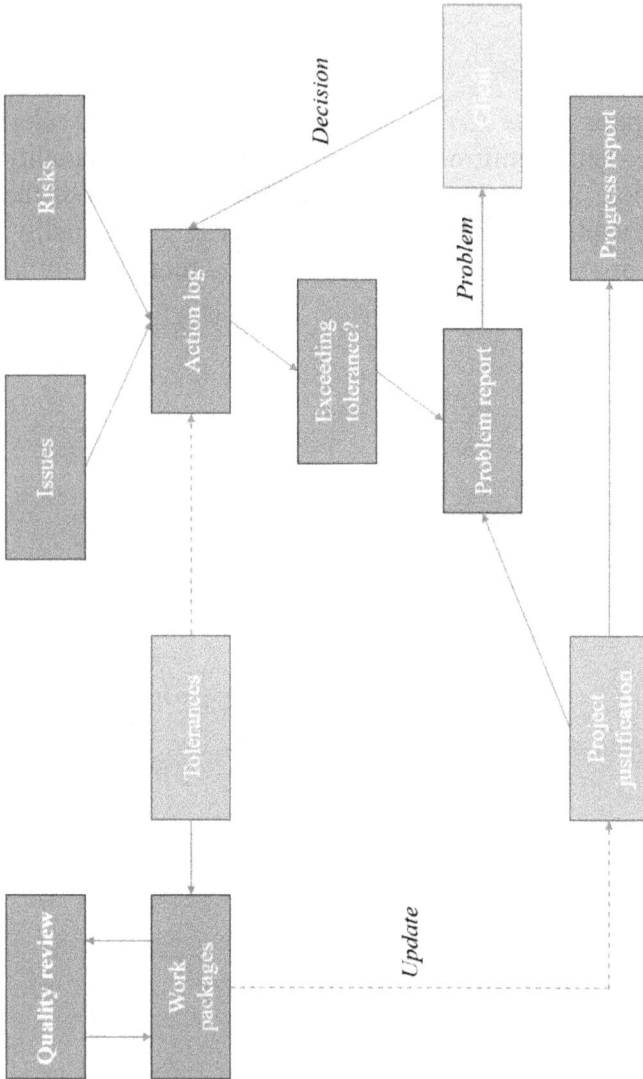

Figure 14.1: The *Create* phase

In summary, the purposes of the *Create* phase are to:

Allocate the work to be done;

- Carry out the work;
- Check the quality of the work;
- Obtain sign-off for the various products;
- Deliver the completed work;
- Keep an eye on risks and issues;
- Monitor tolerance levels; and
- Report on progress.

14.2 Allocate a work package

Work packages are allocated to a team leader or team member based on the needs of the schedule. Work should not start without the permission and authority of the project manager, otherwise it would be very difficult to keep control.

The recipient of the work package must agree with the targets and constraints before the allocation can be considered complete.

The project manager must control the sequence of work packages according to the logical order in which the products need to be created. For example, we don't want to start building the house before we have laid the foundations! The project manager must know what those working on the project are doing, and that the schedule correctly reflects the work and progress.

The project manager will:

- Review the schedule to confirm what work needs to be done, and the time, budget and tolerances available for each work package;

- Discuss each work package with the team leader or team member (recipient) that will carry out the work;
- Ensure the recipient understands the controls to be employed and the quality standards to be met;
- Jointly assess with the recipient any risks or problems and modify the work package and action log as necessary;
- Ensure that any required training material for the users is included as part of the work package;
- Gain agreement with the recipient on work package targets and constraints;
- Allocate and authorise the work to be done; and
- Update the schedule with any adjustments made as part of the agreement.

14.3 Implement a work package

The team member or team leader will carry out the work defined in the work package, including:

- Sharing information with any persons or group defined in the work package;
- Organising and carrying out the quality checks defined in the product description(s);
- Updating the product description and records with details of the quality review results;
- Obtaining sign-off from the identified users that the product has passed its quality check; and
- Returning the completed work package to the project manager.

The work must be done within the constraints and tolerances defined in the work package. Any forecast failure to do this must be reported immediately to the project manager as a project issue (see section 14.5).

The work package may affect or be affected by one or more risks. If the risk owner (see section 7.2.4) is the same person as the one undertaking the work package, this is straightforward. Otherwise, there must be communication with whoever the risk owner is.

During implementation of a work package, the project manager will:

- Monitor the execution of the work;
- Confirm that quality inspections are correctly carried out;
- Update the status of tolerances if there has been any use of them; and
- Regularly review the status of open items in the action log.
- The daily log is a useful place to put in reminders to monitor issues and risks, check the quality of the work and any tolerance concerns.

14.4 Receive completed work packages

The delivered product is checked against the requirements of the work package and confirmation is obtained that the planned quality checks have been carried out and that the product has been signed off by the user(s).

The work package should be updated to record the acceptance of the product(s).

The project manager is responsible for recording the completion and return of work packages and updating the schedule with the results of actual time and resource usage.

As products move through their construction phases, a master copy needs to be stored away and version control used to identify the various versions (see appendix A.6 product version control).

14.5 Controlling risks and issues

A risk is an uncertain event or condition that, if it occurs, has a positive or negative effect on a project's objectives. An issue can be anything to do with the project, either:

- A request for change;
- A question or concern;
- A suggestion; or
- A report of a failure to achieve something that was planned.

The project manager is responsible for the control of risks and issues, although the actual work may be delegated to a team leader or team member. The action log is used to capture, log and categorise any new risks and issues and monitor the status of those that we already know about.

At any time during the project a problem may occur, a change may be requested, a risk may arise or the answer to a question may be sought. If these are missed, it may mean that the project fails to deliver what is required. There must be a procedure to capture these so that appropriate action, if any, can be taken.

The procedure for controlling risks is described in detail in chapter 7.4, but for the purpose of this chapter we will give a summary here.

For risks:

Enter the risk in the action log.

- Assess the effect of the risk on the schedule and project justification.
- Select the most suitable response and plan its implementation.
- Check the communication requirements to see who should be informed of the risk.
- Existing risks should be monitored via the risk owners and remedial action taken if required.

Again, the procedure for managing issues is described in detail in chapter 7.4, but for the purpose of this chapter we will give a summary here.

For issues:

- Enter the issue in the action log.
- Send acknowledgement to the originator of the issue.
- Assess the type, severity and priority of the issue.
- Assess the impact on the schedule, tolerances and project justification.
- Decide on the action to take – accept, reject or pass to the client for a decision.

If an issue is accepted, the schedule and relevant work package with the work required to implement the issue are updated.

14.6 Create a problem report

Reacting to risks and issues will often have an impact on the schedule, such as the time, cost or quality agreed between the client and project manager. If a deviation outside one or more of the tolerance levels is forecast, a problem report should be sent to the client. The project manager is responsible for raising problem reports.

Part of applying the progress control and change principles is that the project manager will bring to the immediate attention of the client anything that can be **forecast** to drive the plan beyond the agreed tolerance limits. This allows the client to stay in overall control of the project. (We have to remember here that the client owns the project justification and therefore, is ultimately responsible for the success (or failure) of the project.)

Using a problem report to escalate issues and risks that threaten tolerances should not be seen as a failure. The client will welcome warnings of potential problems far more than being informed of a situation after the disaster has occurred.

On reviewing the action log and identifying any risks or issues that threaten to exceed tolerance limits, the actions needed to raise a problem report are:

- Check the recommended response to the risk or issue for its impact on the schedule and project justification;
- Revise the recommended response if any problems are found in it;
- Describe the situation, options considered and recommended response to the client in a problem report;
- Check for any stakeholders who should also receive a copy of the report; and

- Take the appropriate action in response to the client's decision, usually an update to the schedule and a new or updated work package. The action taken may require extra monitoring points and perhaps additional reporting on the progress of the actions.

14.7 Report progress

There should be a progress report at the end of the phase (see appendix A.7). The project manager reports on the performance of work so far, including the status of the project, project justification, risks and issues. This is used by the client to decide whether to move to the *Close* phase. Depending on the length of the *Create* phase or, for example, where there is a high-risk work package, the client may request extra progress reports during the phase.

This also allows a review of the status of the project justification. If there is a need, the project manager at this time should update the schedule with the *Close* phase activities for inclusion in the progress report.

14.8 How the principles contribute to the *Create* phase

The project justification principle is used to monitor progress against the expected benefits. Watch for any impact on the post-project review plan and contribute to the assessment of change requests and off-specifications.

Most of the work on the quality of the products is done in this phase. The quality principle affects the product descriptions and work package details. Every product is subject to a quality review.

The planning principle is used where the project plan needs to be updated, especially if it is updated to include a new or revised product following a successful change request.

As the phase name suggests, this is where the creation work is done. Team members need to take instruction, work with other team members, users and stakeholders, and participate in checking the quality of work done. This requires each team member to understand their own role, the role of other members and where authority lies. The project team principle provides this information and structure.

The risk principle is available throughout the phase where new risks are identified or known risks change and require assessment. This is the main phase where risk owners monitor their given risks.

This may be the only phase big enough to warrant the need for progress reports. The progress control principle covers this and any other communication needs.

The *Create* phase is where most change requests and off-specifications will appear and is therefore the phase where the change principle will be most used.

CHAPTER 15: THE CLOSE PHASE

15.1 Purpose

This is the equivalent of the Agile transition phase.

Once all the products have been created, the project team doesn't simply disband and move to other work. A project must come to a controlled end and be closed down in an organised and structured way. The client and development team must agree that a project has met its objectives before it can close and there must be a check that there are no outstanding problems or requests. The development team must also agree with the client that the end product meets the acceptance criteria.

In summary, the purposes of the *Close* phase are to:

- Confirm the products meet their acceptance criteria;
- Handover the completed products;
- Create a project closure report;
- Check the post project review plan; and
- Disband the project team.

Final details are recorded by the team of how long the project took from start to close. Resource usage and cost are compared to the estimates created at planning time, so that a report can be sent to the client on the success of the project. Part of this report will show how much of the various tolerances were used by the project, together with any reasons for this usage.

Any useful lessons learned in the project are recorded for the benefit of future projects. A record is made of any risks or issues that were outstanding at the end of the project and which may require attention during the life of the products, such as change requests that were postponed during the project. Both of these records form part of the project closure report.

There should be an agreed plan to judge achievement of the claimed benefits when it is appropriate to do so. The post project review plan (see section 13.7) was created in the *Plan* phase but may need updating in light of any changes made later in the project.

The completed planning, actual costs and time will go towards a summary of the project performance in the project closure report. The *Close* phase work may also be sufficient to add towards the total project cost and time. The project closure report also states how much of each of the agreed tolerances has been used.

The total actual costs and time taken by the project may affect the level of benefits that were claimed in the project justification, and this may then affect the post project review plan, i.e. has there been a change to the date when some of the benefits can be measured and will they be at the same value expected in the project justification? Therefore, the post project review plan may need to be updated before being submitted to the client.

The action log is reviewed to ensure that every issue and risk has been closed down or transferred to the project closure report.

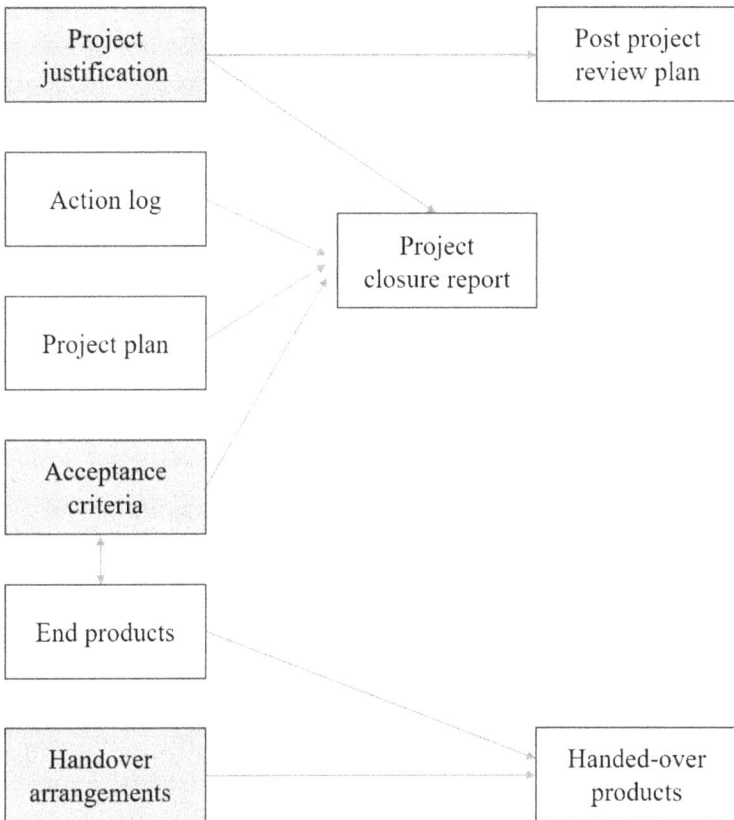

Figure 15.1: The *Close* phase

15.2 APM principles supported

Business need:

The process mainly supports continued business justification. It assesses any benefits already achieved by the project and ensures that there is a reasonable post project review plan to present to the client.

Communicate:

This may be stretching it a little, but the process transfers ownership of the products to the customer and terminates the responsibilities of the client.

15.3 Confirm product acceptance

The product owner must confirm that the project has delivered all the required products to the level of quality defined in the client's quality criteria and that the work meets all the acceptance criteria.

15.4 Handover products

There must be a controlled handover of the project's product(s) and documentation to the users, or those who will operate and maintain them. The development team is responsible but must liaise with the client and users to ensure a smooth and complete handover. This includes:

- Checking that a suitable operational and maintenance environment is ready and prepared to accept the handover;
- Checking the handover arrangements to confirm how the project's products are to be handed over to the operational and maintenance staff;
- Passing the project's products to the relevant operational and maintenance environment;
- Updating the status and location information in the product version control records (see section 8.5);
- Checking if the product records are to be moved to a new site;
- If so, passing the product records to the maintenance

staff; and

- Checking the post project review plan contains measurements for all claimed benefits that cannot be checked until after a period of operational use of the products.

15.5 Create the project closure report

Normally the *Close* phase will be so short that progress reports will not be needed. In exceptional circumstances, the client may ask for a progress report, which will follow the same structure as those in the other phases.

The client and development team must agree that the project has met its objectives before it can close and there must be a check that there are no outstanding risks or issues.

The project documentation, particularly agreements and approvals, should be preserved for any later audits.

The actions performed by the development team to bring a project to a controlled close are:

- Updating the project justification document with the final costs and times;
- Confirming acceptance of the project's product from the client and those who will operate and maintain the product during its operational life;
- Checking that any open risks and issues that might affect the products in their operational environment have been transferred to the maintenance staff;
- Recording any useful lessons that were learned;
- Obtaining agreement from the client that project resources can be released;

- Reviewing the original project mandate, the project justification documents and any changes to it to understand what the project was supposed to achieve;
- Reviewing the project's performance against the project justification in terms of cost and schedule, plus any benefits achieved by the end of the project;
- Assessing the project's performance in terms of its usage of the tolerances; and
- Creating the project closure report.

15.6 Check the post project review plan

The post project review plan, created in the *Plan* phase, shows when, how and with what resources the claimed benefits of the end products can be measured (see section 13.7).

The development team is responsible for checking the post project review plan. It should be checked against all actioned issues to see if there has been any impact on the level of claimed benefits or on how and when measurement of the benefits should be done. If there have been any changes, the post project review plan should be brought up to date.

The development team will probably have been reassigned elsewhere by the time that benefits should be measured. Therefore, the client will be responsible for managing the actual measurement of the benefits, so the development team should pass the plan to the client and ensure that the plan is fully understood.

15.7 Disband the project team

At this point all project work should have been completed and the end product handed over. The team lead should confirm the disbandment of the project team with the client after agreeing that the acceptance criteria have been met.

APPENDIX A.1: ACTION LOG

Remember that these days all documents may be simply held on a computer, rather than on paper.

A.1 Action log

The action log holds a summary of every identified issue and risk. The detail is held on a form, referenced by the action log identifier. Any entries in blue are an example of using the document.

Action log					
Project ID			Project name		
Identifier	Criticality	Date registered	Status	Last reviewed	Owner
R01	*7*	*25/01/2017*	*O*	*15/02/2017*	*Frank*

Appendix A.1: Action log

Status: R=Rejected (Issue only); C=Closed: O=Open; 1–9
Criticality

APPENDIX A.2: DAILY LOG

Daily log				
Project				
Date of entry	**Problem, action, event or comment**	**Person responsible**	**Target date**	**Results**
07/01/2016	*Check status of lease termination.*	*Andy*	*15/01/ 2016*	*Signed termination documents filed.*

APPENDIX A.3: POST PROJECT REVIEW PLAN

Post project review plan	
Version number	*V0.1*
Project	*Health and safety rules re-training.*
End product	*Name of the end product of the project, e.g. trained staff.*
Expected benefit	*Description of a claimed benefit, e.g. staff comply with new rules.*
Pre-project status/measurement	*What was the situation of this benefit before the project began? For example, staff trained to old health and safety rules.*
When to measure	*When can measurement of the benefit be made? For example, project will include testing the staff.*
How to measure	*What is the measurement to be applied? For example, staff required to pass test.*
Resource required	*Are any special skills or tools needed to measure achievement of the benefit? For example, exam questions and answers.*
Responsible	*To whom will this measurement be delegated?*
This is repeated for each benefit.	

Appendix A.3: Post project review plan

Bottlenecks caused	
User views	

APPENDIX A.4: PROBLEM REPORT

Problem report					
Project	*Health and safety rules re-training*	Date	*12/02/2016*	Version no.	*01*

Problem: *Incomplete specification.*

Cause: *New legislation still being produced.*

Consequences: *Cannot finalise training material.*

Options

Option 1: *Close the specification with what is known today.*

Impact: *Possible fine. Incomplete training. Possible failure to fully meet new rules.*

Option 2: *Plan a second project to action new material after the start of this project.*

Impact: *£300. Unnecessary cost of starting a new project. Difficulty in planning team members' future work.*

Option 3: *Continue to accept new rules throughout development and plan for last-minute changes.*

Impact: *No cost.*

Recommendation: *Option 3.*

Appendix A.4: Problem report

Decision		By		Signed	

APPENDIX A.5: PRODUCT DESCRIPTION

Product description			
Product		**Version no.**	

Purpose

This defines the purpose that the product will fulfil and who will use it. Is it a means to an end or an end in itself? It is helpful in understanding the product's functions, size, quality, complexity, robustness, etc.

Composition

This is a list of the parts of the product. For example, if the product were a report, this would be a list of the expected chapters or sections.

Derivation

What are the source products from which this product is derived? Examples include: a design is derived from a specification, a product is bought in from an external supplier, a statement of the expected benefits is obtained from the user or a product is obtained from another department or team.

Format and presentation

The characteristics of the product. For example, if the product were a report, this would specify whether the report should be a Word or PDF document, presentation slides or an email. If the client has a standard for the layout or font size, then this would be mentioned here.

Appendix A.5: Product description

Quality tolerance		

What is the tolerance? For example, the teaching material should cover all the new rules, but there should always be a trainer in attendance to advise on late-arriving legislation or the exam should cover at least 90% of the detail of the new rules.		

Quality criteria	Checked by creator	Checked by reviewer
For example, the training material must be checked against the new legislation by an independent expert.		

Quality method		
What method(s) are to be used to test the quality of the finished product? For example, quality review?		

Quality responsibilities

Role	Responsible individuals
Product creator	
Product reviewer(s)	
Product approver(s)	

APPENDIX A.6: PRODUCT VERSION CONTROL

Product version control	
Version control details	
Identifier	
Title	
Latest version number	
Status	*This depends on the type of finished product. Examples are 'draft/not signed off', 'ready for test', 'complete', 'signed-off/baselined' and 'handed over'.*
Date of last status change	*Date when the status last changed.*
Summary of reason for change	*This may refer to the identifier of the issue that caused the change or may be an explanation.*
Owner	*This is the person who makes decisions on the product's appearance, etc. This is not the creator but the person to whom the product belongs.*
Location	*Where is the product held?*
Copy holders	*Who has a copy and needs to be advised if the product changes?*
Date allocated to the creator	*Date when creation of the product commenced.*

Appendix A.6: Product version control

Relationship with other items	Does it depend on the creation of any other products? Are any other products dependent on this product?
References	Any issues or relevant documentation.

APPENDIX A.7: PROGRESS REPORT

Progress report	
Project	**Period/phase covered**

Major products completed

Any work outstanding: *Anything promised in the previous report that has not been delivered.*

Any problems: *Reason for any failure to deliver and forecast of resolution.*

Issue status: *For example, two issues closed in this period, three issues still open.*

Risk status: *For example, risk of overrunning air conditioning installation removed. Risk of premises not being ready and delaying the office move until after the current contract expires very low.*

Project and phase tolerance status:

Have any tolerances been used? Do any look threatened?

Cost against estimate: *Ahead or below plan?*

Time against estimate: Are we on time, ahead or behind schedule?

Any changes to scope: Have we changed the scope by adding or dropping some major items?

Quality work status: Are the quality checks being done? Do the results show that a good quality product is being developed?

Review of project justification:

Has there been any change to the expected benefits? If so, give the details. Does any change to the expected project schedule or cost have an impact on the justification?

Appendix A.7: Progress report

Forecast: *Plan for the next phase.*		
Signed:	Team lead	Date:
Signed:	Client	Date:

APPENDIX A.8: PROJECT CLOSURE REPORT

<table>
<tr><td colspan="4" align="center">Project closure report</td></tr>
<tr><td>Project</td><td></td><td>Date</td><td></td></tr>
<tr><td>Team lead</td><td colspan="3"></td></tr>
<tr><td colspan="4">Performance against project mandate:

Technical performance against acceptance criteria.</td></tr>
<tr><td colspan="4">Performance against project justification:

Financial and time performance against the figures in the project justification. Any signed off changes should be listed, together with their individual impact.

Any change to the original list of benefits should be highlighted, together with the reasons for the change.</td></tr>
<tr><td colspan="4">Products delivered:

A list of delivered products, together with version numbers.</td></tr>
<tr><td colspan="4">Handover status:

A summary of the transfer of product version control records to the users or operation and maintenance teams, with confirmation from both of their acceptance.</td></tr>
<tr><td colspan="4">Project tolerance status:

An assessment of the project tolerances, how much was used and what caused any impact on them.</td></tr>
<tr><td colspan="4">Issue and risk summary:

A summary of issue management performance and risk management, containing numbers, severity and how well they were dealt with.</td></tr>
</table>

Appendix A.8: Project closure report

Lessons learned:

Details of what went well and what went badly. Any useful lessons can be passed on to future projects.

Follow-on actions:

Details of any open risks that might affect the operational end product and any postponed issues that are being transferred to the maintenance team.

APPENDIX A.9: PROJECT ISSUE

Project issue			
Project name		**Status**	**Open/closed**
Issue ID		**Issue type**	*RC = Request for change* *OS = Off-specification* *C = Concern or question*
Date raised		**Raised by**	
Author		**Attachment**	*If any needed to assist in understanding the issue.*
Issue description		*A description of the issue.*	
Accept/reject		**Reason** **(reject only)**	*The issue will be assessed, and a decision will be made as to whether it is unreasonable with no grounding, and therefore is 'rejected', or it is reasonable and well-grounded, so is therefore 'accepted'. If a decision is made, the 'decision' field of the issue form should be updated accordingly, or if no decision is made it should be left blank.* *If the decision is to 'reject' the issue, the decision field of the*

		issue is updated to 'rejected', with an explanation of the reason it was rejected. The status of the issue is updated to 'closed' and the action log is updated to reflect the same. A copy of the updated project issue form is sent to the project manager and the issue originator.
Priority	High/medium/low/cosmetic	
Impact analysis	*What would be the impact on other products and the project plan if the decision is made to implement any change?*	
Proposed change	*What product/s would have to change? Have any of them already been signed off?*	
Decision		
Decision date		**Signed off by**
Closure date		

APPENDIX A.10: PROJECT JUSTIFICATION

Project justification			
Project ID	Project name		
Version no.	Date		

Project mandate (see attached)

Project approach

Define the choice of approach that will be used to deliver the required products. For example, the method that will be used to provide the solution, such as built by in-house resources, bought off-the-shelf, etc.

Expected benefits	*Describe a benefit that the business thinks will be obtained from using the result of the project? This should be expressed in measurable terms. 'Quicker', 'faster', 'better', 'stronger' and 'more useful' are not measurable terms You need phrases such as '10% faster', 'within two hours of receipt', 'able to withstand a weight of 20 kilos'. In some cases, the business will claim a certain increase in sales or other improvement in their profits. There may be other savings, such as sale of obsolete products/equipment, staff reduction, operational savings, time savings (in monetary terms,*

	for example, a saving of 20 hours overtime each week). In order to measure the benefit achieved, it is necessary to record what the situation is before the project begins. *Costs, savings and benefits are usually shown in a table over a period of time, often three or five years of operational life of the end product.*
Negative impact	*Are there any facilities or earnings that we will lose as a result of creating the new product?*

Client's quality expectations

The quality of the end product in terms of performance, reliability and maintainability that the client is expecting

Acceptance criteria

The criteria that will be assessed against the end product to ensure it meets the client's expectations, and how meeting these will confirm the client's acceptance.

Project interfaces

With whom must the project interface for information or products? With what must the end product interface in its operational life?

Project team structure	*Roles and responsibilities (if there is too much material, this may be a simple diagram with reference to where the detail can be found).*

Appendix A.10: Project justification

Timescale	How long will the project take?
Costs	

What is the total cost according to the project plan? Apart from the project development costs, there may be other costs, such as maintenance costs, re-training costs, costs associated with removal of old products, contract withdrawal costs, etc.

Product descriptions

Tolerances: For example, project cost +/- a percentage or specific figure, time +/- a period of time, scope – is there anything extra for the project to deliver if there is time? What is not a priority that could be dropped in order to meet time or cost constraints? If the project cannot completely meet the quality expectations, are there any limits either side of perfection within which the end product would be acceptable? Are there any expected benefits that the client would be willing to forego or reduce in order to meet the target date or cost?

Risks and issues

Are there any major risks facing the project and its end product? Are there any known concerns or doubts?

APPENDIX A.11: PROJECT MANDATE

One task in the *Propose* phase is to expand on the details of the project proposal. The first four fields: background, reasons, objectives and scope should be in the project proposal, but if not, or if incomplete, these must be completed here.

Project mandate			
Project ID		**Project name**	
Version no.		**Date**	
Background		*What is the current situation?*	
Project objectives		*What is the project to achieve? What will be the major products?*	
Project scope		*What is included in the project scope and what is excluded?*	
Business reasons		*Reasons why the client needs the end product.*	
Constraints and assumptions		*Any constraints, such as ease of use, expected grade and training of the users, specific resources to be used, etc.?*	
Options examined		What options were examined?	
Selected option		Which was the selected option and why? Why were the other options rejected?	

Appendix A.11: Project mandate

Estimated cost	*Rough idea of the total cost.*
Estimated schedule	*Rough idea of the duration.*
The user(s) and stakeholders	*Who will be the users of the products? Who are the major stakeholders?*

APPENDIX A.12: PROJECT PROPOSAL

This is the trigger for a project. It is likely to be incomplete when submitted to the *Propose* phase.

Project proposal			
Project ID		**Name**	
Version no.		**Date**	

Background

For example, sales have risen steadily over the past year. Further increase is limited by stock holding capacity. Current staff are working overtime on a regular basis in order to keep up with increased sales. There is no room for extra staff in current accommodation.

Objectives

For example, increase stock capacity.

More space for extra staff.

Improve working conditions.

Scope

For example, stay in current area.

Increase stock capacity by at least 200%.

Keep current staff.

Business reasons

For example, continued sales increase limited by current capacity.

Staff cannot be expected to continue working permanent overtime.

Appendix A.12: Project proposal

Current telephone system capacity means many sales calls are not reaching us.

APPENDIX A.13: RISK REPORT

Risk report					
Project name	*Business relocation*			Risk ID	*R01*
Raised by	*Frank*	Date Raised	*25/01/2016*	Date Closed	
Risk description	*There may not be enough room under the roof to install the air conditioning unit.*				
Risk analysis					
Probability	*Low to medium*				
Impact	*Serious*				
Proximity	*Immediate*				
Suitable responses				Selected	
1	*Check unit and roof space measurements.*			*1*	
2	*Put in false ceiling.*				
3	*Put air conditioning unit outside in a box against the wall.*				
4					
Risk Owner	*Frank*				
Resourcing	*Frank and air-conditioning company.*				
Reporting	*Daily*				

Appendix A.13: Risk report

Requirements	

APPENDIX A.14: WORK PACKAGE

Work package					
Original date		**Authorised by**		**Allocated to**	
Version no.		*01*		**Date revised**	

Work description

Details of the work.

Product descriptions

Product descriptions of the required products should be attached.

Techniques, tools and procedures to be used

Any techniques, tools and procedures that must be used.

Share information with

Which groups or individuals information must be shared with during the development work.

Dependent products

Any products with which the products of this work package must interact when operational.

Version control

Details of the product identifier(s) to be used. This could be a reference to a document or individual that will have this information.

Time and cost agreements

Appendix A.14: Work package

Start and end dates and cost.
Tolerances *What tolerances have been allocated? Cost and time are the important ones. Quality tolerances will be in the product descriptions, risk and benefit tolerances will usually only apply to the whole project.*
Constraints *Any constraints on the work (for example, language used in the teaching material must be understandable to the least qualified member of staff to be trained).*
Reporting *Frequency and method of reporting to the team.*
Problem handling and escalation *Procedure to be followed when faced with problems.*
Product approval *By whom the products must be signed off.*

Accepted by		**Date**	

FURTHER READING

IT Governance Publishing (ITGP) is the world's leading publisher for governance and compliance. Our industry-leading pocket guides, books, training resources and toolkits are written by real-world practitioners and thought leaders. They are used globally by audiences of all levels, from students to C-suite executives.

Our high-quality publications cover all IT governance, risk and compliance frameworks and are available in a range of formats. This ensures our customers can access the information they need in the way they need it.

Our other publications about project management include:

- *The Concise PRINCE2® – Principles and essential themes, third edition* by Colin Bentley, *www.itgovernancepublishing.co.uk/product/the-concise-prince2-principles-and-essential-themes*
- *PRINCE2® in Action – Project management in real terms* by Susan Tuttle, *www.itgovernancepublishing.co.uk/product/prince2-in-action*
- *PRINCE2 Agile™ An Implementation Pocket Guide – Step-by-step advice for every project type* by Jamie Lynn Cooke, *www.itgovernancepublishing.co.uk/product/prince2-agile-an-implementation-pocket-guide*

For more information on ITGP and branded publishing services, and to view our full list of publications, visit *www.itgovernancepublishing.co.uk*.

To receive regular updates from ITGP, including information on new publications in your area(s) of interest, sign up for our newsletter at *www.itgovernancepublishing.co.uk/topic/newsletter*.

Branded publishing

Through our branded publishing service, you can customise ITGP publications with your company's branding.

Find out more at

www.itgovernancepublishing.co.uk/topic/branded-publishing-services.

Related services

ITGP is part of GRC International Group, which offers a comprehensive range of complementary products and services to help organisations meet their objectives.

For a full range of resources on project management visit *www.itgovernance.co.uk/shop/category/project-management*.

Training services

The IT Governance training programme is built on our extensive practical experience designing and implementing management systems based on ISO standards, best practice and regulations.

Our courses help attendees develop practical skills and comply with contractual and regulatory requirements. They also support career development via recognised qualifications.

Learn more about our training courses and view the full course catalogue at *www.itgovernance.co.uk/training*.

Professional services and consultancy

We are a leading global consultancy of IT governance, risk management and compliance solutions. We advise businesses around the world on their most critical issues and present cost-saving and risk-reducing solutions based on international best practice and frameworks.

We offer a wide range of delivery methods to suit all budgets, timescales and preferred project approaches.

Find out how our consultancy services can help your organisation at *www.itgovernance.co.uk/consulting*.

Industry news

Want to stay up to date with the latest developments and resources in the IT governance and compliance market? Subscribe to our Weekly Round-up newsletter and we will send you mobile-friendly emails with fresh news and features about your preferred areas of interest, as well as unmissable offers and free resources to help you successfully start your projects. *www.itgovernance.co.uk/weekly-round-up*.

EU for product safety is Stephen Evans, The Mill Enterprise Hub, Stagreenan, Drogheda, Co. Louth, A92 CD3D, Ireland. (servicecentre@itgovernance.eu)

www.ingramcontent.com/pod-product-compliance
Lightning Source LLC
Chambersburg PA
CBHW060406220326
41598CB00023B/3040